Wiking

CW01022841

Henk Kistemaker

Wiking

A Dutch SS-soldier on the Eastern front

CONTENTS

A WORD OF THANKS.

.

I would like to thank all the people that volunteered to help me in correcting and editing the manuscript.

At the time the publisher received the manuscript I had the help from:

Tony Edwards,

Sven Zimmerman,

Simon Wright,

Anthony Mitchell,

Bruce Morris,

Mike Janse,

Del Elson,

David Walker,

William Carpenter,

John Johnson,

Mick Daly and

Ronnie Goldwater.

I would like to thank all those men above for their time and patience

Peter Kistemaker

1

PROLOGUE

The protagonist of this historical narrative, Henk Kistemaker, was born in Amsterdam, Netherlands, November 4th of 1922. He volunteered in 1941, as an 18-year-old, to join the Waffen SS, a German military unit. After his training, he was sent to the Eastern front to fight the Russians, while serving with the 5th. division-Wiking. There he fought until 1945 in some of the most bloody and gruesome engagements of the 20th century. During his first two years he served in the infantry but later became part of the famous 'Panther,' panzer divisions.

By the end of the war, he was a twenty-two-year old, tried and tested, veteran.

After being repatriated to the Netherlands, he was charged, convicted and sentenced to 5 years imprisonment for volunteering, in times of war, to fight for the enemy military. In 1948, he, along with many other convicts, was granted amnesty, and pardoned, after Queen Wilhelmina of the Netherlands abdicated the throne in favour of her daughter Juliana.

Due to Henk Kistemaker having been a Waffen SS member, there were precious few work opportunities made available to him in post war Netherlands. As a result, he returned to Germany to live with his pen pal girlfriend, whom he'd met in 1943. He lived with her for 5 years in Klingenberg, near Wurzburg and in 1953 they were married. In that same year, they returned to Holland and in 1956 their only child was born, a son named Peter.

While trying to get work in the Netherlands, Henk found it necessary to lie about what he did during the war. He would speak honestly about those days only to a close circle of relatives or friends.

Although he felt he was a loner, he managed, by self-study, dedication and hard work to climb the social ladder. During the 1990s, at the request of his son Peter, Henk began writing his memoirs of those war years and took about three years to do so. In this way, he recorded his unimaginable experiences for his son and for posterity.

Henk Kistemaker died from an illness on March 15th 2003, at the age of eighty.

This narrative was written for family records, not with the intention of publishing. Although there was a time lapse of 5 decades between the war experience and Kistemaker's committing it to writing Henk was gifted with a photographic memory. "It was phenomenal," Peter recalls, "all names, dates, and experiences were etched in his memory from the day they occurred, until the day he died."

Peter also affirmed his father researched and refreshed his memory by consulting institutional records and war diaries. The result was that Henk Kistemaker became a historian of considerable knowledge about the war on the Eastern front. Knowing this, it is remarkable that he never wrote about the Jewish persecution, death camps such as Auschwitz or Sobibor, the Nazi ideology or the infamous Einsatzkommandos at the Eastern front. To Peter, Henk Kistemaker stated: "All that was out of our field of view. We did not concern ourselves with it."

Peter wrote: "My father was not a man to plead guilty or acknowledge involvement in any of this. That was not in his character. Do I believe him? I don't know."

Later investigation by a Dutch historian, Evert-Jan van Roekel, proved that the Wiking division was involved in war crimes on Jewish people. The historian, having read Kistemaker's writings, expressed doubt that he or his comrades knew nothing about this. "Even if he didn't participate, it would be unlikely, he didn't know of the atrocities," according to the historian. Of course, he knew, after the war, what had happened; he couldn't deny that. But he didn't feel responsible because he wasn't involved.

To his son he allowed: World War II had its foundation in the treaty of Versailles agreed by the Allies and The League of Nations after 1918. Germany was stripped of much of its sovereignty and had its empire in the form of overseas colonies confiscated and re-aligned with other nations, such as Britain. It was also levied impossible financial reparations that brought the nation to the brink of bankruptcy. He added, with raised eyebrows, England and France declared war on Germany after it invaded Poland but didn't declare war on Russia, which invaded Poland at the same time, but from the east. 'Why?' he asked.

Henk writes a lot about the number of war's victims, but says nothing about its cause. Even though he fought for four years of his life in an evil system, he wouldn't say anything critical of Nazi Germany. When his son asked him about it, his answer was short: "I had no political involvements, neither was I interested in the person of Hitler. We didn't talk about him. We just did as we were ordered and a soldier never questions during wartime." (Befehl ist Befehl or an Order is an Order)

According to Peter, his father was an admirer of Nazi Germany discipline. There was respect, order, discipline and regularity; all things his father admired. Peter believes his father lived by the rule: If I don't go against it, I won't get into trouble.

Henk Kistemaker wouldn't accept and didn't believe, his comrades of the Waffen SS committed war crimes. His belief was based on the fact: 'He never saw any such acts take place in his division and, the Wiking division was never charged or convicted of any war crimes. We now know this not to be true. About many things we will never know exactly what happened. "Do you know how many soldiers and civilians, friend and foe, were killed by the Russians?" he asked. "You know that nobody ever got convicted for that? Do you know what kind of bad things the Americans, French and Polish army did? Nobody will ever be convicted for that. The winner never gets convicted, it's the loser who gets his place on the stake."

Images in Steven Spielberg's movie Saving Private Ryan brought sighs of satisfaction when he saw portrayals of Americans shooting German soldiers after they had raised their hands in surrender. 'Thank God', he uttered, 'At least he's got the balls to show this atrocity, also a war crime, the likes of which happened on both sides.'

Although Henk Kistemaker didn't talk about political motivations, he must have been subject to Nazi propaganda during his training as a member of the Waffen SS. To his son he confided:

"At my parents' home in Holland I listened to the stories of sailors from the German navy. In the city, we found pamphlets that asked us to join the Waffen SS to fight Bolshevism. Excitement and adventure lured me to join them. Anything was better than staying home being unemployed. On top of this, my father was very pro-German and member of a pro-German political party, the NSB."

When Peter asked; "If you were looking for adventure and excitement, why didn't you volunteer with the allies?" he was thoughtful for a few seconds and then replied: "I don't think my father would have appreciated that."

Peter said: "I understood that. Having a different opinion to the family in that time was not common. He was expected to choose what his father thought best for him. Has my father participated in war crimes? Did he see it happen? Did he know about it? I will never know, but I give him the benefit of the doubt on this issue."

The rest of his natural life, Kistemaker had no doubts at all about his Waffen SS membership.

According to his son, he would have done the same again in the same circumstances. His army period was the best period of his life, he told his son. Even though he lost numerous friends and suffered severe hardships, he always said that the camaraderie in the German army was the best. "We literally went through fire for each other and were prepared to die for each other. You will never find a spirit and attitude like that in civilian life."

After the war, he missed that 'Band of Brothers feeling' he

experienced over there and found it nowhere else. Later, after he was pensioned off, he went to meetings of the old Waffen SS members to relive those times again.

Peter continues the story: "Out of curiosity, I went along with him a couple of times. I found a lot of old men, talking and exchanging memories of a time from which they never knew if there would be another day for them. During those meetings, I never saw Swastikas or Nazi flags. They didn't talk about Hitler, only his many dubious strategical decisions, that had affected their lives."

The most notable thing in Henk Kistemaker's story is the lack of emotion and compassion. Peter, noticing this, asked his father about it. "He couldn't let emotions in," Peter recalls, "because if he did, he wouldn't be able to write anymore. He managed during daytime to switch off but, sometimes, during the night, when memories haunted him in his sleep, he woke up, shouting, they attack us, they attack us! They are coming from the left side! Only to wake up, be calmed down by his wife and went back to sleep again."

"Sometimes he couldn't 'switch' off. In the story at the end of the book, when the young blond soldier boy, dies, while holding my father's hand, he would cry."

His son recalls: "When I looked at his face, at that moment, I saw the emotion and the pain of that particular memory. It was like all his lost friends and comrades were embedded in that young boy's death. I felt his pain and I felt sorry for him."

After Henk died, his son, lovingly, gathered all those memories, put them in sequence and kept them, thinking, someday, maybe somebody will want to publish them. Even though many elements are missing in this book – Repentance, Guilt, Contemplation, Reflection – I think, for a publisher, this story from Henk Kistemaker, is fascinating.

The Publisher.

2
HOW IT ALL BEGAN

Every story, every life has a beginning. And so it was the same for me. So let's begin with how it all started.

I was born on November 4th 1922 in Amsterdam-North. I was the 5th and youngest child of my family. By the time I came into this world our family had already lost a little boy, due to the Spanish Flu epidemic of 1918. Besides this little brother, that I never got to know, I had three older sisters.

By the time I wrote this journal, my parents and all of my three sisters had already passed away.

I do not have much recollection of my early child years. I remember one thing though, when my sisters took me out in the stroller, one of the wheels came off, causing the stroller to fall sideways and with me inside rolling off a dike.

I sustained no injuries here, but I still remember that event very clearly.

I couldn't have been no more as(than) 2 or 3 years old.

Also I remember, at elementary school, we had a teacher who drove a B.S.A motorcycle and he took the children for a spin around the block, that was awesome.

I also remember, there was an award for who was the best in mathematics and I always won that.

Mathematics has always been my favourite subject at school. Later in life, after the war, I became an accountant. But many interesting events had to happen first, before I came to walk on that road.

After my time at elementary school, I went to the MULO (high school) and after graduation, I wanted to find a job. This proved almost impossible because around this time, the famous crisis years (Great Depression) of the thirties with high unemployment occurred, a job was very difficult to find.

So I stayed at home. But by doing nothing, I annoyed my father and aggravated he took me to the port of Amsterdam, where he found me a job as steelworker. This was not really what I had in mind, but it kept me off the street. Working during the day, I started to go to school in the evening. Hopefully, with getting more and better education, I would increase my chances on finding a job in the near future.

At this school, I was trained to be a ship radio telegrapher and radio technician.

Little did I know back then that, because of this education, I would spent 3 years of my life in a Panther panzer during the (World War2) as a radio-operator. How strange the twists and turns your life can make?

The high school I graduated before previously, didn't have the level that was required to enrol in this type of education, so I also completed HBS (Highest level of high school at that time).

I took lessons in mathematics, geometry, logarithm, English and also German language classes.

It took me more than 2 years, before I was ready to do the examination, scheduled for June 1940.

Like many of my classmates, we were even before graduation already contracted by Shell as wireless operators. But due to the unforeseen circumstances this was never going to happen.

In May 1940 the Germans attacked the Netherlands and within 5 days the Government of the Netherlands surrendered.

The school was closed and the exams would never take place. So without a diploma, I was out on the streets again.

During the days, I found a job at an inland shipping company, but because of the war, there was not much work to do there at that time.

Let me tell you a little bit more about my mother and, especially, my father.

The memories I have about my father and mother are as different as night and day. Their characters were complete opposites, like chalk and cheese.

My mother was a gentle, loving, conservative and caring woman and my father was rough, tough, progressive, adventurous and not scared of anybody or anything. My mother came from a family with educated people an intellectual background and my father came from a poor working class family with little or no education. I think the only reason they got married was because my mother fell pregnant with his child and my father's strong sense of duty to take care of what he had started. He was true to his word and come hell or high water, he always provided for his family, in any way he could and by whatever means possible.

My father, in contrast to my mother, had little formal education. I remember how he taught himself 'difficult' words by reading the newspaper with a dictionary in his hand. He wrote down every word he didn't know the meaning of and looked it up in the dictionary. Over time, his knowledge and understanding of the Dutch language increased. My mother, on the other hand, stayed at home to take care of, what would eventually become, a family of four. My father tried everything to earn money for his family.

I remember that at this time he was already a member of the NSB (de Nationale Socialistische Beweging or the National Socialistic Movement) a pro-Nazi Dutch political party, and he decided to open a fruit and vegetable stall in Amsterdam.

This particular area, known as 'Kattenburg' was mostly inhabited by people that voted or belonged to the Communist Political Party. They were, like, the political archenemies, of the members from the NSB, which happened to be the political choice of my father.

In hindsight, it wasn't really a very clever business venture to start with, a NSB member owning a shop in an area full of Communist Party members.

My father, once he had made his mind up, wasn't easily discouraged or distracted and was not a quitter under any circumstances.

For him, as a businessman, he put aside any grievances he had about political choices and opinions, or even religion. He just wanted to do business.

He even hired a local guy to drive his delivery truck because he didn't have a driver's licence.

This guy was also a member of the Communist Party but my father didn't care about that.

'If he can drive the truck and is a good worker, then he has the job', he told me, when I questioned his choice on people who worked for him.

I admired that about him, but I also had the sense of trouble lying ahead for him, and it was to come sooner than expected. Sometimes the emotions between the people who lived there and those of my father rise to a pitch of high tension.

His shop was at the end of a long narrow street, a so called cul-de-sac and he had to walk through that long street to get to his store.

One day, they even threatened to kill him if he came to work at the stall.

My mother almost died from fright when she heard about all those threats, but not my father.

'They are all big mouths, because they belong to a group', he said, 'and on their own, they are cowards, scared shitless to make a move by themselves. I am not backing off from those people.'

He went to his tool shed and took an axe, swung it over his shoulder and walked out of the door.

'What are you doing?' I asked with surprise, 'they will kill you for sure if you walk along that street again.'

He shrugged his shoulders, turned around, looked at me and said: 'No, they won't. Let them try it. The first one who comes close to me, I will bash his brains with this axe' and his eyes looked at the tool on his shoulders and then back to me.

I knew he would do it and so did they.

That day he walked all alone along that long and narrow street just to open his store.

Although he was a small man, my father had a strong and muscular build and with an axe on his shoulder he was not afraid of anything or anybody.

As it turned out nobody confronted him or even dared to come close. He was right, the majority of those people were cowards and could only be brave by hiding in the crowd.

A small man, but with big balls, that was my father, I can tell you that.

He taught me that day what the word courage actually means.

In the end, sadly the shop couldn't survive.

Nobody had the guts to risk a personal confrontation with my father, instead they just boycotted his shop.

Sometimes they would fire a gun at his fruit and vegetables and I would find the bullets, lodged in the oranges. Then the inevitable happened. Due to the boycott, he did not have enough income anymore, he had to fire the man who drove his delivery truck.

The poor man, not being one of the brightest souls of the planet, immediately hanged himself after he lost his job. The newspaper from the Communist Party 'De Waarheid' (The Truth) published a whole article about what they said was the scandalous behaviour of my father.

The headlines in their newspaper called him 'Kistemaker Moordenaar' (Kistemaker Murderer) blaming him for the death of one of their party members.

After this, my father had to close his store permanently and he applied for a job in the port of Amsterdam as a steelworker.

He never again started a business of his own, but for me it marked him out as a strong individual, not afraid to fight for his rights and somebody who didn't give up easily.

It turned out later that I had more in common with him than I first thought.

My parents, being members of the NSB (Nationale Socialistische Beweging or National Socialistic Movement) political party(that was pro-Germany,) were being raided on May 10th, 1940 by the police and accused of giving light signals to German planes that had flown overhead the same day the Germans invaded the Netherlands. Until this day, I still have no clue what kind of signals we were supposed to have given these planes? It would seem that they only needed an excuse to take us in and arrest us.

As NSB party members, they considered us 'dangerous' and the whole family was transported to the police station, where everybody was searched. The men had to hand over, belts and shoelaces., so they wouldn't hang themselves. I could not believe they thought I planned to do that.

Because my brother-in- law was not a "party member" they let him out, with a kick in the ass as a farewell gift, that is.

From the police station, they transported us to the local Market Halls.

Here we met hundreds of other party members. For me, it was obvious that the government had planned this already a long time before, otherwise it would be impossible to execute this operation with such short notice.

Next they transported us to the harbour area and all of us were gathered there in empty barracks.

They quickly filled up to capacity. We were guarded by the Dutch navy militaries (Marines) and if you needed to go to the toilet a guard would accompany you. Being 17 years of age, I thought, it was all quit exciting.

On May 15th 1940, the Netherlands surrendered to the Germans and after hearing about that fact, one of the marines shot himself through his head. I still wonder why? What do you hope to accomplish with that? I never, ever, even in the most difficult of times that lay ahead of me, had the thought of taking my own life. Later, at the end of the war, many fanatical Waffen SS members followed Hitler's example and killed themselves. Not me, where there is life, there is hope.

Suddenly, after my country surrendered to the Germans, we were free to go home.

Arriving home, the neighbours, who at first initially had been very hostile towards us, now started to be super friendly.

Our windows were not smashed anymore and their attitude changed into subservient and friendly behaviour.

Right up until the war's end, this attitude went on, but after the end of the war, the whole hatred towards us, would flare up once again. Even more aggressive than before the war.

After the Netherlands capitulated, the German navy would dock their fleet in the harbours of Amsterdam where my father worked. My father spoke the German language fluently because he grew up in the eastern provinces of the Netherlands, just a stone throw away from the German border, and even went to a German school in his elementary years.

He invited the German navy personnel into our home.

Those guys told me all about their adventures and experiences. I was mesmerised by their stories.

In those days we didn't go anywhere. The only world I knew was the little world I grew up in, and that was the northern part of Amsterdam.

It looked like one great adventure to me, to be a soldier like them and travel the world and see all those different people and places.

By that time the SS started to recruit soldiers by hanging posters in Amsterdam.

On it, it stated; 'Come and join us, to fight against Bolshevism'.

Well, that appealed to my father. First of all he believed in a Great German Empire, but second of all, he hated the Communists.

'Join them son', he told me and so I went to the drafting agency of the German Waffen SS.

At that time, the physical test they let you do, was very strict. Later on in the war, when they desperately needed more soldiers, they adjusted it downwards.

First of all the doctor measured my skull to figure out if I was Arian enough.

I passed that one and all the other test as well and got an approval to join the Waffen SS.

February 28th of 1941, I had to report myself in the Dutch town of The Hague, from where onward I would be transported to Germany by train.

My father wanted to accompany me to the train station to say goodbye to his only son. The moment the train started to roll out of the station, he brought the Hitler salute with outstretched arm and I was actually glad nobody knew that this was my father because, to be honest, I felt a little embarrassed.

I really enjoyed the train trip. It was the first time in my life I had crossed the border. Before the war, working class people like me, didn't have the money to travel anywhere.

After a beautiful scenic train trip we were unloaded In the Elzas area. Next we were transported by trucks to the barracks in Sennheim,

Germany. The first training facility we would be in.

Being only used in eating Dutch food, I really had to get used to the food the Germans gave me.

In the beginning I disliked it, but after a while it grew on me. Now, I love it.

For a fortnight we stayed in Sennheim. No weapons were handed over to us at this time. We only had to physical exercises and marching, day in and day out.

Near Hamburg we received further training, where I got assigned to 1st Battalion Germania infantry. It was with this unit I would go to Russia.

After another 14 days, the train brought us to Klagenfurt in Austria. For the first time in my life I saw the mountains with their snow-covered tops. It was such a beautiful landscape.

In Klagenfurt, I saw Hitler for the first time. We were ordered to control the crowd, who reacted over enthusiastically as Hitler passed by.

From a short distance I saw the man, the one who I pledged my honour and my life to, passing in his Mercedes convertible through the crowd.

In the barracks in Klagenfurt they gave us intensive weapon training and mastering. I liked that part, but I disliked the teargas exercises. They put you in a room with teargas and after a while you had to change your filter and you always ended up with painful, teary eyes.

One day, the whole company stood in line, names were called.

In Germany they called me Kiestenmacher, instead of Kistemaker and I heard them call my name.

It turned out, they classified me to a SMG unit, so I had to be transferred to the city of Graz, also in Austria.

There we got, first of all a technical training, to learn all the ins and outs, dos and don'ts about the MG34 (one year later we got the MG42).

We had to walk into the hills (only 400 meters high, but still) carrying the gun carriage (a tripod) that weighed a stunning 20 kilo's. On itself 20 kilo's is not too much, but walking uphill you will feel every kilo of that on your back.

On top of that, once in a while, they would shout: 'Take cover' and you had to let yourself fall to the ground. Every time, doing that, the tripod would bounce against your steel helmet, and that started to get pretty annoying. On our way back, the whole company would be exhausted.

One morning I awoke, not feeling well. I had a sore throat and fever on top of it. They treated me like I was a leper! A good soldier never is sick and if he is, he doesn't show it, they told me.

I wanted to see a doctor, but before they let me see one, they instructed me to scrub the floor of the bathroom first. I felt sicker with every moment. At last they let me see a doctor and his diagnosis was laryngitis.

They admitted me to a hospital. After a few days, being fever free again, I returned to my unit.

Never again would I call myself sick again. Let somebody else scrub the floor, not me anymore.

Next we went to the city of Vienna, were we trained more.

Meanwhile it was June 1941, and suddenly they woke us in the middle of the night. We had to be up and ready in 30 minutes. The whole

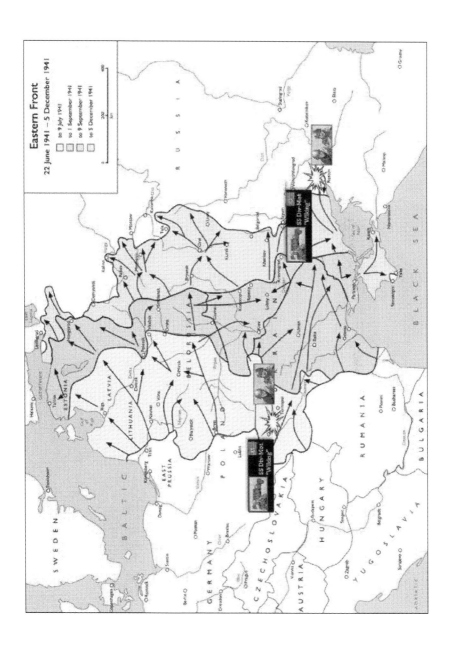

unit boarded the trains again and now we were transported to Poland. This was new territory for me and also for many of us.

Poland looked, in comparison with Germany and Austria, untended and poor.

Again we went to barracks, but this time they had no running water, so all the soldiers had to wash themselves in the nearby river. Luckily it was June and not December.

The pressure we felt before, during all those weeks of training started to wear off.

They gave us more slack. Now our whole unit contained trained and fit men with the skills of artillery, engineers, SMG (Heavy Machine Guns) and LIG (Light Infantry Guns, like mortars).

Before they would transport us to be a part of the oncoming start of operation Barbarossa on June 22nd 1941, we had to complete a three days march of 120 kilometres. Fully packed, that is.

On the third day, our commander walked next to me and asked me why I looked like I was worried?

I wasn't, so I didn't understand why he asked me that. He said my face looked like I was worried.

Now I understand what he meant. When I'm preoccupied in my own mind, I look a little glum.

My face is like that. I can't help it. Besides that, I could also be a comedian comes the time. But more importantly, I am not likely to sit down and give up on anything. And those character traits, I needed desperately for the years to come.

Operation Barbarossa was about to begin.

On the 22nd June 1941, the full scale Operation Barbarossa was launched. Russia was under attack by three German armies, North, Middle and South. I was part of army South and our main objective would be the oilfields in the Caucasus. Well, we almost made it. During our advance, we went through a deserted village and there we found a lot of weapons, left behind by the Russians. They probably left the village in a hurry and didn't bother to take all their weapons along with them.

Of course, being young guys, we were curious about these weapons. It was like being a kid in a toy store. Some of those weapons were so different from ours. They had a riffle, with a long barrel, it looked like it came straight out of the First World War. We found mortars, a PAK (Anti-tank gun) ammunition and hand grenades. We also found explosive bullets amidst the stacks of ammunition. These were illegal and not allowed according to the Geneva Convention.

But hey, you think the Russian gave a damn about that? They even shot our convoys, wearing the banners of the Red Cross. They killed wounded German soldiers in the hospitals and shot, many, Waffen SS soldier, on the spot after they surrendered. This war would be a brutal one, with no mercy or respect given from both sides.

I suddenly heard a big explosion and somebody was screaming. One of my comrades was rolling on the floor, holding both of his hands in front of his eyes.

What happened? One of the other soldiers found a Russian hand grenade and took a closer look.

At one point the grenade started to make a hissing sound and in a panic he threw it away. It landed just in front of the feet of the, now severely wounded, soldier as it exploded.

I remember, the wounded guy was Belgian and he lost the eyesight in one eye and his whole body was full with shrapnel, but he survived. He got full military disability and for him, the war would be already over, after it just had started. In the meanwhile trucks arrived, and together with another four man, we were classified to the 1st Germania battalion. Nobody, at that time, could know how tragically the fate of this battalion would be. I was the only one that being issued to the 4th company of those four man. They named us the 'heavy' company because it had all the heavy weapons like eight centimetre mortars, and the SMG (heavy machinegun)

The trouble started immediately on the next morning. It was on the 18th of July 1941. We had to take a little village, lying straight ahead of us, named Taraschtscha. Early in the morning we started, after our artillery had softened up the enemy with a 15 minutes barrage of fire. I was part of a SMG unit. A unit like this contains five men and I was the last one, number five or also called 'Schutze Arsch' or Tail Gunner. It was my task to get the empty ammunition boxes of the MG back (behind the frontline) and replace them with full ones. I could be promoted in the SMG team, but that happened only if number 1 (the actual shooter) gets wounded or dies. Number 2 becomes number 1, number 3 becomes number 2 and so forth. Besides the ammunition I had to carry, I was also fully loaded myself. I carried two boxes with six mortar grenades, 60 shots of ammunition for my own rifle, a couple of hand grenades (the so-called potato mashers), a collapsible shovel, a gasmask and a gas tent to give protection against gas attacks, a bread pouch, a piece of canvas and a trench knife. Altogether, it must have been around 25 kilos of weight I had to carry around on the battlefield.

Luckily, we didn't have to walk that far into the field. Our mortar, had already made his stand, and started to 'spit' out his grenades to the guys at the other side of the front line. We called it 'spit out' because you threw the grenade into the tube, it would then hit the ignition plate, that would ignite the grenade and it would launch itself out of the tube. A very simple, but effective weapon. The grenades had a very light ignition mechanism, therefore the grenade would immediately explode as it hit the ground, sending shrapnel low across the ground. If you lay down, shrapnel would penetrate you all over your body, so you better get up then, but that was the moment the SMG crew was waiting for. Once you were standing up, you became a perfect target for the thousands of bullets the SMG could release every minute. Hell, you had to hit the deck again, but now those damn mortars started to ruin your day again. The Russians attacked as one big group of screaming and shouting men, running into the fire of mortars and SMG. This 'strategy' could only be successful, if you didn't care about the amount of casualties and you had enough soldiers to do it.

Well both of them applied to the Russians. Higher command didn't care how many men would be killed, they had plenty of them 'in stock'. If you refused to attack, it would mean being shot instantly and if retreating it would be the same procedure. The life of a Russian soldiers had no value at all to Stalin.

Our attack, in the same situation, would be: spreading out your soldiers over a large area, then, randomly, a couple of soldiers would jump up, advance and drop down again. Before the machine-gunner from the Russians, even could aim, his target would drop already out of sight.

Then at random again, another couple of men would jump up and drop a couple of meters further. By doing this, the advance would proceed with a minimum of casualties. Also, because of the men being wide spread over the field, the grenades couldn't inflict too many casualties at one time.

We didn't have those amounts of manpower the Russians had, so our strategy was a more conservative one. It was also psychological it was very important to give the soldiers the idea that, by their training and skills and strategy, they would have a higher chance to survive. Nobody, I guess, wanted to be on a suicide mission. At least I wasn't.

During the shooting, I heard sergeant Sack calling my name. 'Henk, fetch us a couple of boxes of grenades from the back'. The means of transport for this was a motorcycle with sidecar. It was operated by Walter Kordes and he waited, a couple of hundreds of meters behind the line of fire, hiding behind some bushes. Walter would bring you to the ammunition supply and take you back again. He would be killed in action in December 1943, but of course and lucky for him at that time, he wasn't aware of this. If everybody would know, what lay ahead of them, most of them would have turned around and run away, I think.

You can only motivate soldiers in a war, if they think, they have a high chance of survival.

Walter also brought trench coats for the night and supplied us with food from the field kitchen.

After he brought me back, he went into hiding behind his bushes again and I started to walk back, with the boxes of ammunition for the mortars. All around me, I heard, those whizzing sounds, but I didn't give that any thoughts. Until sergeant Sack shouted; 'Hit the floor damn, HIT THE FLOOR! Do you have a death wish?' I followed his order immediately, and, now crawling over the floor, made my way back to our unit. I felt embarrassed, in acting so stupid like the rookie I still was.

Sack still hadn't finished his monologue to me: 'Never EVER walk straight up at the front lines, you understand?! Look to your comrades as an example!' He was right, everybody, when walking, was in a bent over position. I was one of my first survival lessons and I'm glad I learnt it.

Survival was a combination of skills, experience and good luck, as I was about to find out the coming years.

We moved further south east, to the town of Smela (Smila). We wanted to take that city, but the Russians weren't prepared to gift-wrap it for us. The city was therefore under heavy defence.

I noticed that the Russian soldiers were masters in making, almost undetectable, foxholes. I mean, you hardly could see them, until you almost stumbled into them.

At Smela we lost our sergeant Hohn. One of our lighter (5 centimetre) mortar units asked him for his assistance. They had, we so called it, a 'Rorhkrepierer' that means, the grenade didn't come out of the tube. The ignition probably hadn't worked and now it got stuck in the mortar tube. A very dangerous and precarious situation, as it would soon turn out.

Hohn tried to get the grenade out of the tube and, while he was doing this, the grenade exploded and killed him instantly. We felt sad, because he was a good sergeant and a nice guy.

At the start of Operation Barbarossa we advanced with lightning speed. We conquered huge territory and it seemed we were invincible. But the Russians didn't give up. They retreated and retreated, luring us into a country that was on scale beyond our imagination. You know, I had never left the Netherlands before in my life. We lived in

Amsterdam North and that's where I spent most of my life. We didn't travel. So everything I saw, everything I experienced was an eye-opener for me and it left me amazed. How the people in Russia lived? They were very poor and lived in small houses, if you could call it a house anyhow. It was most of the time, in our eyes, a shed.

One day we surrounded a little village. It seemed already abandoned and we got the command to check every house for booby traps left by the enemy and/or the enemy.

This is a tricky mission and we lost many comrades due to booby traps. So we were on the top of our nerves with every house we checked.

My group contained 5 infantry man, including myself. Until 1943 I served in the infantry. After that I got transferred to a Panther panzer, but back to the story now.

We entered a house that seemed abandoned. Some of us carried a rifle, some of us a pistol, ready to use it in an instant. We checked every room, opened every door of every closet until…one of us opened the door to a hall closet and got confronted with a little boy, maybe 7 or 8 years old, pointing a revolver at him. In a millisecond of time my comrade reacted and pulled the trigger of his rifle. We heard the sound of one shot, which sounded very loud in the little house. We all went to our comrade to find out why he shot and at whom? We found him pale white looking in the hall closet. On the floor was the body of a little boy, crumbled on the floor with a big hole in his chest. His face was turning grey and we knew he was beyond help.

Now the four of us started shouting at our comrade: 'Why, for crying out loud, did you shoot a child!' One of us said. 'Look next to his body', the soldier said, 'he pointed that revolver at me, what else could I have done?' We saw the revolver on the floor of the hall closet, next to the body of the dead little boy. 'Couldn't you just had knocked him out instead of immediately shooting him?' another one wanted to know. Not one of us felt 'proud' of killing this little boy, although we knew he was armed and probably would have shot our comrade if he would have been able to react quicker.

'I don't think any of you would have reacted differently', he stated in his defence. In retrospect I think he was right. War is an ugly monster. You act, on impulse, due to your training. One second to late could mean you would be the one lying dead on the floor. We finished the 'cleaning' of the little village without further incidents, but until now I can still see, as if it happened only yesterday, that little dead boy with that bullet hole in his chest, on the floor of the hall closet somewhere in Russia.

Some memories stay in your mind forever.

The next city to take, was a tongue breaker called: Dnjeprodzerinsk It lay positioned on the banks of the massive Dnjepr River. We had to cross that river in the coming days. Some of the Russians tried to escape, using rafts, to cross the river, but our artillery became the party-pooper for them.

Three of those rafts were blasted out of the water. Not many Russians made it to the other side.

Thousands, and I mean THOUSANDS of them became POWs and wandered in long big lines behind the frontlines towards a POW camp. They also left tons of weapons and ammunition behind for us. It is always nice to get a present, isn't it? We now had some time to spend and we started to catch fish in the Dnjepr River but not through the use of a fishing rod, OH NO!

We threw hand grenades into the water and after the explosion of one grenade, six or seven fish came to the surface. Very lucrative, but it was also forbidden to use your own hand grenades, but what the hell, nobody noticed. Our next and dangerous mission would be in crossing the Dnjepr River. Italian engineers were already busy in make pontoon bridges, so we could advance to the other side.

3
THE ITALIANS

The next city we reached was Dnjepropetrovsk, a much bigger city than the ones we had previously passed through.

With a deafening howl and a massive explosion the grenades from the Russian artillery came over and landed behind our lines.

Luckily the impact of these grenades was far behind us, so we had a brief moment of rest.

However, this was a selfish thought, because now they exploded in the lines of our comrades who were in that area.

In the beginning of September we crossed the Djnepr river ,which was no easy task.

We were waiting in the streets of a little village until we got the command to cross.

Meanwhile the streets were full of shrapnel from the exploding grenades of the Russian artillery.

They were pretty accurate because at the other side of the river was a Russian artillery school, so they knew the distances to their targets in that area and lost no time in making their calculations.

Suddenly I heard the order; 'Come on, Get up, Move, We are crossing the river now.'

We walked in line with 10 meters between the soldier in front and the soldier behind, because of the danger from flying shrapnel.

The moment we reached the banks of the river, someone shouted; 'Take cover!' we dropped our bodies in a split second into the soil.

The warning was not a moment too soon as suddenly we were attacked with bombs from overflying Russian planes. Luckily most of the bombs landed on the houses behind us and in the river. only a few hit the pontoon bridges we were constructing to get us over to the other side.

Construction of the bridges was carried out by Italian engineer troops. Their job was to mend the damage to the pontoons caused by the bombs and grenades that were falling all around. I didn't envy their job at all.

After about one hour of waiting, the pontoons had been sufficiently repaired to allow us to get to the other side and the command sounded once again: 'Go, Go, Go!'

We ran as fast we were able to as we were carrying full combat gear. The sooner, the better as the bombs were still falling and the artillery kept shooting grenades.

We had to pass the Italians engineers on the pontoons, sometimes we tripped and stumbled over the tools that were lying around everywhere.

At last we reached the other side and exhausted, we dropped to the banks of the river. We weren't allowed any rest. 'Come on. Get Up, Move on!' was the command, so we dragged our bodies further inland, away from the river. This was because of all the shrapnel flying around, so we had to get away as quickly as possible out of the area.

We Jokingly called situations like this: 'The air is full of iron today'

Behind a couple of deserted houses we finally stopped and caught our breath.

At last we could rest and get some sleep, as far as I could remember we didn't have to stand guard, something that rarely ever happened.

The next morning they brought us breakfast, well if you can call one piece of dried old bread a breakfast? But when you are hungry, and we always were, you eat everything ..... that old dried bread tasted delicious. Our planned advance for that morning was postponed because the Russian artillery had laid down heavy fire on the sector we were supposed to be going to. It was the heaviest barrage I had ever experienced. It was breath taking and deafening at the same time. Later that day, the Russian artillery stopped firing. At least into the sector we were heading for, that is.

The moment we started to advance, the German artillery behind us, started an immense barrage of fire, clearing the area we were going to. It made our advance easier. Shortly after that the first Russian soldiers who had surrendered came into sight. Immediately I picked one out of their lines and commanded him to carry the mortar grenades that I was carrying. Judging by his expression, he was not happy at all with his new task, but what could he do?

Now the warning came that we would be crossing a minefield. I hated mines, they made me very nervous knowing that I was going into a mine infested area. We stopped and put our mortar up. We had to wait until the minefield was cleared by our mine clearing group.

All in all on this day and the next we managed to advance quite a bit. We secured our bridgeheads. More and more troops followed the path that we had already covered.

Finally we arrived at the spot where we would stay. Not a very comfortable place, I have to say. In front of us was an area, covered with dead horses and Russians, and we had to camp in the middle of it.

Me and my mate Muller 17 (Muller is such a common name in Germany, we gave them numbers to tell them apart) started digging our little bunker. We covered it with planks and a mattress we had found and then covered it with a lot of sand. It wouldn't do us any good if we got a direct hit from a grenade or bomb, but for shrapnel and bullets, still flying around occasionally, it was okay.

We had hardly finished our little shelter when the Russians started firing again. They wanted to take back all the land we had conquered. However we didn't agree with that, there had to be a fight. War in a nutshell.

The sequence of an attack is for most of the time the same: first the artillery starts to fire, then the planes start to drop bombs and when that's all done, the infantry would try and advance. You could always tell when it was time for the enemy infantry attack, because the artillery would move their fire further back, out of the sector where their troops were advancing, so they would not kill their own men.

This time my duty was with the mortar unit. The combination of mortar fire and heavy machineguns was almost impossible for the enemy infantry to overrun. They needed armoured cars or tanks to clear the path. Luckily for us, they didn't have any of these. The Russian losses were staggering and they didn't succeed in claiming back the territory they had already lost.

One evening, still in this sector, we got a message from command. We would be relieved pretty soon! Help was on its way. After all those days, we were suffering from battle fatigue.

Surprisingly the troops that would take our place to secure the sector turned out to be Italians.

They started to mingle amongst us, talking Italian which no one could understand. But also they showed us many nude female pictures. Pornographic pictures.

Nowadays that may seem pretty normal, but back in those days it wasn't. Being 18 years of age I had never even seen a naked woman or even a picture of one. For me, it was awkward and embarrassing.

We were allowed to pull back to our previous sector, which now had been secured by the Italians.

After our first, proper meal, we all fell into a deep sleep.

It was not even midnight, we were all awake again because of an alarm.

What happened? The Italians were on the run and the Russians occupied the sector we had just left to them to secure. It turned out to be a Russian advance infantry group of just twenty men! THAT was what scared the Italians off? We had to go back and, as tired as we were, we had to secure our old sector yet again. But that meant no relief for us.

From that day on I hated the Italians, as soldiers they were no good.

They couldn't hold Africa, and if we hadn't helped them conquer Greece in 1941, the Greeks would probably have conquered Italy.

If you want soldiers, beside the Germans, with a good fighting spirit, you needed Norwegians, Finns, Danes, The Dutch and/or Belgians. With them you could form a good team of soldiers.

We were back, holding our old sector, but the dead horses and Russians had started to decompose now. It was pretty hot at that time and the smell of rotting meat was all around us. Anybody, who had never had to smell this, can call himself very lucky because the stench was awful. You wanted to throw up constantly. In the end we had no other option than to bury the decomposing bodies.

All over the field there were the craters of bombs and grenades, so that made the job much easier. We put handkerchiefs to our mouths and noses to mask the incredible stench. We dragged the dead Russians, with a rope around their legs to the craters and tossed them in. Once full, we covered them with soil. All around us, everybody was doing the same, so that we could clear our sector from this hellish smell. Normally I would check the bodies for the cause of death, but in this case, with all the flies and maggots crawling on top of them my curiosity was gone.

Dragging these bodies to their graves I noticed that they were not young soldiers, like in our army. Most of us were teenagers, or in our twenties, but these guys looked old. Saying that, I have to say that because of my age at that time, 18 years old, everybody older than, let's say 35, looked old to me.

Probably their families would never find out what happened to their loved ones.

Of course the Russians had a sort of 'Dog Tag' around their necks, but because of their superstitious beliefs, that if you wore them, you would be killed, many of them just threw them away.

It's no wonder that millions of Russian soldiers were never identified and ended up in nameless graves. Family and friends would only receive the message 'Missing in action' keeping up their hopes that one day, they would be back again.

Our 'Dog Tag' was an oval one consisting of two equal parts containing just the division and registration number of the soldier. The top part stayed with the body and the lower part was broken off and sent back to Central Administration.

Yeah, the Germans were good in that respect. Everything had to be filed and ordered and written down.

Sometimes I think they lost the war because of the fact they focused too much on small details and perfection. I mean, take our panzers for example. Everything was welded to perfection, inside there were hooks and storage places for EVERYTHING. It was 'comfortable'. If you compare that to a Russian T34: the welding was very sloppy, and in the beginning they didn't even have radio communications. Sometimes the driver's seat would be a wooden crate. I actually saw that. But…. they were producing many more than the Germans. We couldn't keep up with their production capacity. If we lost one panzer, nothing came back in return. If we destroyed 100 T34's in one day, next day, they came back with another 100. You couldn't beat that, and it was, in my opinion, one of the reasons for the downfall of the Third Reich.

Our commander told us to make a defence line with three MG 42's. Our intelligence expected an attack by a large group of Russian infantry.

During my time in the Germania infantry I was a member of a machine gun crew that was equipped with the MG 34 and later with the MG 42.

It was one, if not the fastest, machine gun of the second WW and was feared by all our enemies. They fired an astonishing 1200 to 1800 rounds per minute. The barrels became so hot that from time to time we had to change them, using heat resistant gloves.

We made three 'nests'. Two, that would engage the enemy immediately when within range, the other being a 'silent' one, meaning it would stay silent, positioned on the flank, until the enemy would walk unexpectedly, into their line of fire.

We prepared our trenches and stacked plenty of ammunition because the MG 42 uses a lot of it.

Most of the time, we worked together with 'granatwerfer' a.k.a. mortars.

We fired our machineguns in a wave like pattern from left to right and back again. When the enemy hit the ground to escape the murderous fire, the mortars would start firing and the moment the grenade hit the soil, it would explode sending shrapnel low over the ground.

So if the enemy didn't want to be punctured by shrapnel ,they had to get up and start running. At that moment the machineguns would open fire again, mowing them down. They hit the floor and the mortars would start again.

It was very, very difficult for our enemies to get through a defence like that.

But the Russians had many soldiers. They didn't care how many were killed.

We heard them coming. It started with a loud Hurray, like a thousand throats, yelling and they started running at our line of defence. The moment they came within range, the two MG nests started firing.

You wouldn't have believed it, if you hadn't seen it.

Like being struck by a giant hand, we saw the first line and then the second line of attackers fall to the ground.

But they kept on coming. They pushed on and on, climbing over their wounded and dead comrades coming closer and closer to our line of defence.

It was now getting very tricky, so the third MG started firing and wiped them out from the flank.

Still they kept coming and now the first victims were falling within 10 meters of our trenches.

We had no time to think of anything else. We worked completely mechanically due to our strict training. Shooting, loading, shooting, loading, changing the barrel, shooting, loading. It went on and on and on, like that.

The first Russians tumbled dead or wounded to the left and right side of our trenches.

If they didn't give up pretty soon, we would be in big trouble.

Suddenly, the attack stopped and the enemy retreated, with what was left of their own line of defence.

We finally allowed ourselves to breathe deep, in and out. Oh my God, this was really a close call. A big sigh of relief.

Now we had time to look around. The battlefield was like a massacre.

Hundreds of dead and wounded men lying everywhere.

Carnage.... No medical care. The wounded in the field would die overnight anyway.

Nobody was coming to their aid.

It was the moaning and crying that got to the best of us and reminded me that it could have been me. Lucky again.

Suddenly we heard moaning to the left of us In our trench. We moved carefully to the sound and found a Russian soldier with a shot through his stomach.

In the frontline a shot through your stomach meant, most of the time, a certain and very painful dead.

Only if you had immediately access to medical help, that could transport you to a field hospital to get first aid, you stood a very small chance.

But here? Out in the middle of nowhere?

No way that guy would have survived. He was still conscious and looked at us like he wanted to kill us, which was probably the reason why he was here in the first place.

Sad for him, that we stopped him from carrying out his murderous intentions.

All the hate in that face as he looked at us, the enemy.

So close to his goal, but he couldn't do anything to us anymore.

We decided to leave him alone. He would die overnight anyway. Just like most of the wounded on the battlefield in front of us.

Slowly, during the night, the voices and the moaning stopped.

Because we were always sleepy, we slept on turn, until daybreak came and woke us up.

To our surprise the guest we had in our trenches, our 'friend' the Russian, was still alive. We were amazed.

His face, besides showing extreme pain, showed still the same amount of anger and hate.

This was one strong guy! We were impressed. So, out of respect for his strength, we called for a 'sanni' or sanitator or medic.

On the other side of the line they asked us who had been wounded.

We told them it was a Russian with a stomach wound.

He stayed a couple of seconds completely silent on the line, then;

'Come again? You want us to come and get a wounded Russian?'

I've never heard so much unbelief in that voice in my life.

'Yes', we answered, 'so please come and get him.'

Not long after that the medics came with a stretcher, lifted the Russian onto it and went away. Still shaking their head in disbelief.

We don't know if he survived his wounds or not and if he did, would he survive as a POW? We never heard of him again. But he earned our respect.

That's for sure.

Note: even after the war my father kept up his grudge against the Italians. Whilst many people went on holiday to Italy, we never did. Other people visited Italian restaurants, not us, no way. Until his dying day he kept his disappointment about their combat mentality. He told me many times: 'They have big mouths, make a lot of noise, and show off like they are Julius Caesar themselves, but when push comes to shove….forget it, they are gone.' And his face would show his disgust when he spoke those words.

Me? I like Italian food, I like the Italian country and their old rich culture, but then again, I never had go to war with them. So what do I know?

4

SNIPERS AND HONEY

We were getting nervous, the line we had been holding already for a couple of days was close to the edge of a forest.

If there had not been a war going on, it would have been a beautiful spot to relax and enjoy the view.

So… what caused our nervousness?

Well, in that forest was an active Russian sniper, and that guy was good, very good.

We couldn't spot him, and he had killed and wounded already several of our men.

They say that the only way to get a sniper is with another sniper, so we radioed command to ask for a German sniper.

They sent us a guy and we explained to him the situation, and where we thought the sniper could possibly be located.

The forest was dense and lush, so we wondered how the Russian sniper could even get a good shot at us? His marksmanship was extraordinary.

The German sniper heard all our stories about where and when the shots were fired, and in which spot our men had been killed, or wounded.

He nodded after hearing all this information, like he had a good mental picture of the whole situation, and left for the forest.

We watched him entering the forest and soon he was gone.

We waited two days, and still he hadn't appeared.

In the meantime, we lost another comrade and another one was badly wounded. Could the German sniper have become a victim of that Russian sniper too?

Then, on the morning of the third day, our sniper came out of the forest. He walked slowly.

We didn't see any signs of success from his body language.

Maybe he couldn't find him, and the Russian guy was just too good?

When he was within range we shouted:

"And? Did you kill that son if a bitch?"

He nodded, but still no sign of triumph, so we started to wonder what was wrong with him.

Surely, he must be feeling proud?

Now he was back in our lines and he jumped into the trench.

"Yes", he said, "I got your sniper, but it wasn't what I expected it to be."

"Why? What", we all started to ask him.

"It was a young woman", he said.

Our jaws dropped in disbelief, and now we wanted to see her with our own eyes.

Saying this may seem awkward to you, but we were all young boys and curious. Not so specifically, because it was a woman, although in this case, a female sniper triggered our curiosity, but more that we wanted to see how and where he got her.

Sometimes, after a battle, and when everything was settled down, we walked over the battlefield.

In all my years in the war I have seen every part of a human body been hit by bullets, shrapnel, explosions and whatever other killing devices you can think of.

On a battlefield, you find, of course, many dead people and most of the time the cause of death will be obvious.

People who lost arms, legs or their head, weren't a big medical puzzle to figure out what had killed them, but sometimes we found people who had 'nothing'.

At least that's how it looked to us.

Why were they dead? They seemed 'complete'. There were no missing body parts and there were no outer signs of gunshots or wounds by shrapnel.

They were just dead. Dead without a cause and that puzzled us. Sometimes we turned them over and investigated the body, like a medical detective. Every so often you could find a tiny little hole, somewhere on their body, and we guessed that tiny hole must have been what killed them.

A lot of times we didn't find any clues and puzzled, we would talk to our company doctor about this.

He explained that sometimes a heavy, nearby explosion can cause severe internal damage because of immense air pressure, and the victim dies because of internal bleeding. No external signs are to be found then.

One day we heard that one of our comrades had died because of an acute appendicitis. We were stunned. Flabbergasted. Somebody died by natural causes? That never happened! You die by a bullet or by shrapnel, but natural causes? Never! Our whole perspective about what was 'normal' or not shifted by our experiences in the war.

When I joined the war, I was still 18 years old and very naïve.

I didn't think I could be killed. I had received the best training and I was in the best army of the world.

The enemy would suffer losses of course, not us.

Until I found out that my comrades, who also had that same 'best training' I had, and were in that same good army, died around me.

During my four years on the Eastern front, I learned quickly that death could come as a surprise.

Sometimes you just have 'bad luck'. There is nothing you can do about that.

But most of the times, I learned, you can influence your faith to the good.

After a while I learned the sound of every grenade coming in at us.

I knew where it would approximately land and if I had to worry.

If you had the time to live and learn, you grew slowly into a veteran at cheating death.

By the time I was 22 years old, I had spent 4 years in one of the most horrible wars ever and I had survived.

It was a combination of skill and luck. Good luck.

I lost many good friends in those years, sometimes only by trivial unnecessary accidents, and I survived.

'Why me?', I sometimes asked myself.

But back to the sniper story now.

We were walking through the forest, our sniper leading the way. After a short walk he stopped and said: 'Here I killed her.'

We looked around but didn't see any trace of a body.

'Where is she?', I asked.

He pointed with his finger to the tree, that was standing next to us, and we all looked up.

There, strapped to the tree, about 10 meters from the ground, was the body of the Russian sniper.

She had strapped herself to the tree, so even if she had fallen asleep, she couldn't fall out of the tree.

From that view point, she would have had an excellent view of our lines.

One of us climbed into the tree and cut her straps with his trench knife.

She fell out of the tree and landed like a sack of potatoes, in front of us.

Now we could take a good look at her.

The shot from our sniper had hit her straight in her heart, and she must have died instantly. All in all, it was an incredible shot by our sniper.

Her face was unharmed, and we saw that she was a very beautiful young girl about our age. Most of us were in our late teens or early twenties and so was she.

All of us went silent. Nobody spoke a word, and nobody felt exhilarated.

'Now you know how I feel', our sniper said.

'I expected to kill a male enemy soldier, man to man. His skill to mine. Instead I killed a young woman and it doesn't feel good. What was she doing in this war anyhow?'

We all felt the same. It was confusing. We knew we had to kill the enemy, but we expected them to be male.

The rules of this war had changed once again and not for the better. After the war I was told the Soviet Union had around 2000 female snipers in their service.

Until now we had regularly received shots from the other side, from where the Russians had their positions.

Of course, we returned their fire, take a little and give a little, isn't it?

But one day something was wrong. At first, we didn't know what was happening, there were no shots fired anymore! An earie silence hung over the field. If you are constantly in an area with shooting and grenades, then suddenly all that noise stops, its awkward. You are not used to complete silence anymore. What was happening? Maybe the Russians are planning a major offensive? Our reconnaissance guy informed us not much later, that the Russians were gone!

So, we got the command to take advantage of this situation and move more to the east.

It was a long convoy with all kinds of trucks driving eastwards, making a big dust cloud, because the roads were unpaved and just dirt, like most of the roads in Russia.

It slowed you down, but still we managed to conquer a lot of territory in a reasonably short amount of time.

This dust cloud was visible miles ahead and we hoped it wouldn't attract enemy fighter planes.

In the beginning of the war there were not much Russian fighter planes left, but once in a while, some of them appeared on the horizon and attacked us.

I never understood their tactics by the way.

When they approached us, they started shooting at the flank of the convoy.

Our planes always attacked the length of a convoy. That made much more sense, because it causes more casualties to the enemy.

The Russians flank attack only caused minor damage or casualties.

They never changed this tactic, to our great pleasure, until the end of the war.

Our trucks had, in the back, two benches for soldiers to sit on.

On every bench seven men could take a place, so the truck transported 14 soldiers.

My spot was behind the cabin of the truck.

In the cabin itself we had the driver and our Oberscharfuehrer, (I think it's called an N.C.O in English), Hugo Schramm.

At our feet they stocked all our personal gear and ammunition. To my right side there was a provision box.

At that moment it contained only dry bread, and because I was hungry I took a slice of the bread.

On my opposite side, facing me, sat Muller 17, (because of this being a common name in Germany we gave them numbers to tell them apart).

He saw me taking the dried old bread and said: 'You want some honey to go with that?'

Flabbergasted I answered: 'Honey? You have honey?'

'No', he said, 'but Oberscharfuehrer Schramm has' ,and he showed me the jar with honey, in the corner of the provision box.

'We can take some. He will never notice', Muller 17 said to me.

I hardly needed any convincing. Besides being always hungry, we also craved for sweets.

So, a couple of minutes later we enjoyed our bread with a thick layer of honey.

But we had miscalculated our whole 'honey' operation, because the temperature was cold at this time of the year. The honey wasn't running and didn't equalize itself in the jar.

No, instead you could clearly see the fingerprints of the ones who took some honey out of

the jar, and at the time we didn't give it any attention.

After driving for the whole day, at dusk we arrived at a little village.

This would be the place to make our quarters.

After that we had to clean all our weapons. This was a rule without any exceptions.

We were just starting to clean our weapons, when we heard the angry voice of our Oberscharfuehrer Schramm: 'Everybody in line. Attention!'

All the men followed his command and within a minute the lines were formed.

In front of us was our angry looking Oberscharfuehrer, and he shouted: 'Who took honey out of my jar!?'

Well, everybody in our truck knew who did it, and besides that, if nobody would report himself, the whole group would be punished, and you didn't want that to happen.

Muller 17 and I looked at each other, and then stepped forwards.

We were immediately given a punishment exercise.

We had to crawl through the mud, climb over a haystack, run around the house and so on.

The Russian women of the village looked on in amazement at what those strange 'Germanskis' were doing?

The other downside was that we got the worst times to cover at night watch.

Never at the beginning or at the end of the night, but always in the middle of the night, when you are in a deep sleep. But our luck was about to change….

November 1st of 1941 we were in an area of the Ukraine with villages that had German names like Marienheim or Gustavsfeld.

I don't know if they changed those names after the war, but at the time they were called that.

In one of those villages we saw dogs running from one village to another and back again.

One of us, with more experience in Russia, told us these were dogs that brought messages from one village to another.

He grabbed his riffle and tried to shoot the dogs, but the distance was too far, so he didn't hit any one of them.

However, all that shooting triggered a reaction from a group of Russian infantry, that was obviously hiding in the village, and they started to open fire at us.

Before we knew it, we had to take cover and bullets were flying all over the place.

Muller 17 and I hit the ground, then suddenly Muller 17 pointed in front of us and said: 'Look, there lies Oberscharfuehrer Schramm.'

I looked in his direction and saw the one who had tormented our lives over the past few days.

'Shall I shoot him through his leg?', Muller 17 said with a big grin on his face, and before I could do or say anything he had aimed and shot.

Nobody, except me, saw him do that.

The bullet went right through the leg of Oberscharfuehrer Schramm.

With all that shooting around us, nobody would ever know we did this.

Shortly after the shot, we heard somebody shout: 'Two volunteers to get Oberscharfuehrer Schramm. He has been wounded.'

Muller 17 and I looked at each other, we grinned, and volunteered to transport Schramm out of there.

When we reached him, I could see the bullet went through his right thigh.

I had my canvas with me and we rolled him on it.

He was a heavy guy and we had to be careful because bullets were still buzzing around us.

We had to drag him for 20 meters with all the strength we had, before we reached a spot behind the line of fire.

Now we could lift him, and we carried him to a motorcycle with sidecar and put him on top of it.

And that was it. For the time being we were freed from his torments towards us.

Months later, when he came back to our unit, his attitude completely changed.

In his mind we were the ones that saved his life, when he was wounded.

Nobody else volunteered to get him out of that firefight, only the two of us did, and we got his eternal gratitude for that.

Never again did we have to do night watch, never again did we have to do dirty jobs or dangerous missions.

For as long as I served under him in the 'Germania' division, (until 1943, when I was transferred to the Panther tanks), I fared well!

After the war, and after I reached my pension age in 1987, I started to attend the meetings of my old comrades in Germany from the 'Germania and Wiking' divisions.

I met up with Oberscharfuehrer Hugo Schramm there again.

Muller 17, as far anybody could tell me, never made it through the war.

So, I was the only one who really knew what happened at that time.

On one occasion, under loud cheers from all my comrades, I handed him a jar of honey to give him back what we had, a long time ago, taken from him.

His nickname, since that event, was Hugo Honey, and until his dying day he never knew that it was Muller 17 who put a bullet in his leg and sent him to a hospital.

I thought it was for the better this way.

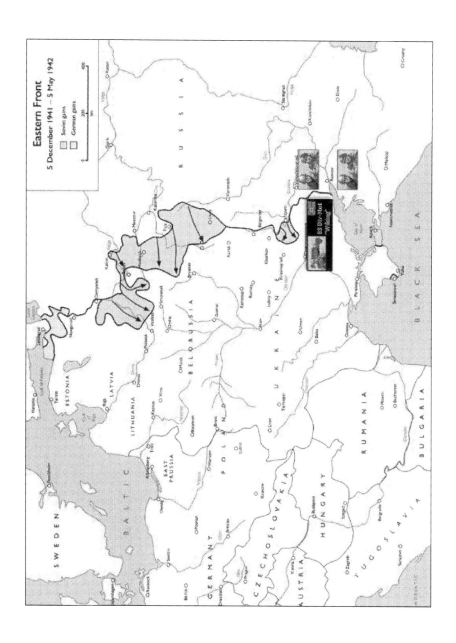

5
WOUNDED

We found our quarters in a stretched out Russian village. My guard duty didn't start until after midnight, so I got some sleep first. I was gone in a minute.

Suddenly somebody kicked me hard under my boots and startled me awake. 'Get up! Alarm!' was the message that I heard.

It turned out that we had a heavy exchange of fire with some Russian infantry.

They wanted to make their quarters in the same village as we did. They didn't know that we had already occupied it.

Our guards heard them coming, but started shooting immediately when they didn't get the required password answered.

Although it was pitch-dark, I mingled myself into the firefight.

We could only see where the Russians were positioned if they fired their riffles.

The flash of that fire gave us the direction to aim.

It didn't take long for the fight to end, or for the Russians to retreat.

Probably they would try to find a less hostile spot to spend the night. They left their dead comrades behind.

The next morning we could actually see what damage had been done.

Dead Russian soldiers were found even in the village. They must have passed our guards without either side noticing the other.

The bodies were quickly stripped of their clothes by the people of the village, especially the boots were favourite items.

The civilians didn't show much respect for their dead soldiers as far I could see.

That day, we also experienced being targeted by a, so called, 'Stalin Organ'.

On a truck they had, I guess, around 30 rockets which they fired at once.

The screaming and howling of those rockets was more terrible and scary than the accuracy of them.

All of the rockets missed us completely and landed next to the village.

Therefore nobody was hurt, but it scared the hell out of us, so the commanders decided it would be better to move out of the village and we made our quarter somewhere in the fields.

As I was busy making my foxhole, they ordered me to get coffee for the group.

Our kitchen , they told me, must be in one of the nearby villages.

Meanwhile night had fallen and, again, it was pitch-dark.

With six kettles, to fill with coffee, I went on my way.

After a short while I felt lost. Helpless I stopped in this amazing wide open field.

While standing still the kettles didn't clatter against each other anymore.

Suddenly I heard voices. Maybe I was closer to the village than I thought?

The sound of voices and footsteps approached me and suddenly fear gripped my throat, because the sounds I heard were NOT German at all.

Remembering the events of the night before, I ducked into a small ditch on the side of the road and made myself as small as possible to avoid detection.

This was just in time, because out of the dark shapes appeared and they, as I already feared, turned out to be Russian soldiers.

With my heart pounding like crazy from fear of being detected I held still and didn't move a muscle.

After a while, which seemed like an eternity to me, the last Russians passed my hiding place and I waited until I could hear no more sound before I decided to get up.

Suddenly somebody came running towards me.

I froze, raised my riffle and shouted: 'Stoj! Rukki Werch!' (Stop. Raise your hands).

These were the first Russians words I had learned and they proved very useful in that moment.

The person in front of me stopped, raised his hands and I could see it was a young Russian soldier of my age.

I commanded him 'Idi Sjuda' (Come here).

He came towards me and he was armed with a light machine-gun.

I took it from him, because it was better than my riffle.

I felt as proud as I could be. I just had captured, singlehandedly, a Russian soldier!

Suddenly I remembered that I had lost my sense of direction. I decided to ask the Russian.

I told him: 'Come here, Iwan.'

But the Russian pointed at himself and answered: 'Pan, ja Igor, nix Iwan' (Sir, my name is Igor and not Iwan).

Well, now that we are acquainted, I asked him where the German troops were positioned.

My Russian knowledge was very rudimentary, so I draw a line in the sand and pointed at it:

'Wot Russki? Kuda Germanski?' (Here are the Russians, where are the Germans?)

With a very happy face, glad he could help me, he pointed me into a direction that was 90 degrees different to the direction I had been taking.

Suddenly I got scared.

Maybe he would bring me directly to his Russian comrades and that would mean that I would end up as a POW or worse?

But what could I do? I had to take a gamble and follow him wherever he would bring me; This would be either to become a POW or to get coffee?

After walking for half an hour, a light flare raise into the air and I heard a German voice saying;

'Stop! Who is out there?'

I answered with the password for that night and we were allowed to approach.

The guard looked at the Russian and me and you could see the surprise in his face. 'Where the hell did those two guys come from?'

I asked him which company this was and he told me it was the 3rd.

I had to be at the 4th company, so he pointed me in the right direction.

I had to leave my 'friend' Igor behind, filled up my kettles with hot coffee and went back to the 4th company.

There they wouldn't believe my story about capturing the Russian soldier until 3rd company confirmed it the next day.

On November 18th we made quarters in a village near a river.

They told me, that I could stay in the house of a Russian doctor.

Nothing fancy about that. His house was the same aa those of all of the other villagers.

The first evening I was playing chess with another comrade in a barn.

The doctor provided us with the board and pieces.

Playing chess is, I think, the number one game in Russia. Many Russians play it and the doctor and his wife were standing next to us watching the development of our game.

In the meanwhile the Russians firing their artillery.

We thought we were pretty safe. The impacts were far away, so it didn't worry us at all.

Suddenly I noticed, through the window on the left of me, a bright flash of light.

I didn't even hear the explosion.

The shockwave threw me to the floor and I started to hear a whizzing sound in my ears.

As I got up, I noticed that the wife of the doctor was dead.

She had been hit by some shrapnel and it had killed her immediately.

Neither my comrade nor the doctor had any injuries.

I had some minor wounds in my neck.

At our medical centre, they removed some splinters from of my neck and covered the wounds with bandage.

Next day we had to move on. I wore my bandage with pride.

This was the first time that I had been wounded! I didn't know at that time I would be wounded two more times before this war ended.

But being lightly wounded, meant that you survived. Many of my comrades were not so lucky.

In February of 1942, the landscape was covered with a thick blanket of snow.

The snow was so soft, that we couldn't use the sleds anymore.

We had to carry all our equipment ourselves.

I carried two boxes with grenades (22 kilo) and later, on top of that, I also had to carry the barrel of the machinegun, because somebody fell ill.

The landscape we were walking through, they called Balka's in Russia.

It was a sloping landscape that gave you cover from enemy fire, but walking up and down those hills, fully packed, through the snow, can make you exhausted in no-time.

The group was guided at the front by a friend of mine, his name was Karl Bender.

Suddenly we heard a big explosion and loud screaming.

As I approached the spot of the explosion, I saw my friend Karl on the ground.

He had stepped on a mine and was terribly wounded.

He had lost his foot and the flesh of his lower leg was completely torn away by the explosion, exposing only bare bones. An awful sight.

We tried to stop the bleeding, but he died as we were busy trying to save him.

I was completely shocked. This hit me hard, very hard. I lost a good friend.

We lost comrades before, but that was different.

This was a friend of mine and emotionally this hits you like a ton of bricks.

Later in the war, getting more experienced, I learned that 'making friends' only meant I would lose them again.

So to protect myself from going, time and again, through the grief of loss, I started to adopt a more superficial approach to new recruits.

Yeah, I would talk with them, become friendly, but never wanted to go that far that they would become my friend.

Before you know they were killed and you had lost a friend again.

How much grief can a person take before it gets the best of you?

I didn't want to find out.

It was cold, freezing cold. Although this winter we were better prepared than one before. Our first winter was unimaginable and horrific, because high command were not prepared for wintertime war, so no winter clothing had been provided to us. Being an infantryman at that time, it meant you had to deal with temperatures around -40 Celsius. Imagine that out in the open and you can imagine many of my comrades froze to death. They fell into a sleep from which they never awoke, just to be found next day as a frozen human popsicle.

Now we had winter clothing, so no complaints about that. But we were hungry. Starving, I might say. The supply lines from our logistics service were stretched out beyond their limits because of the fast advances that we (still) made.

So we had lack of two things: sleep and food. Whenever one of those was available you would get it, in whichever form or shape it came didn't matter. We slept everywhere where we could and we ate everything that we could lay our hands on. At least, that's what I thought about myself. Until….

One day we were engaged in heavy combat with a Russian infantry group.

We managed to kill most of them and the remaining forces fled into the nearby woods or surrendered.

Both options were dangerous, because many times, if they fled, they were executed by their own political communist officers or, when they surrendered to us, they sometimes got executed also.

Why? Because many times we didn't know what to do with all those prisoners and sometimes, when you just lost a couple of your own comrades and the enemy raises their hands to surrender, you are so full of anger, you just shot them.

So now, after the battle, we looked over a wide field covered with snow and you could see the bodies of all the dead Russians still lying there, frozen solid.

I was together with a comrade, as a civilian he was a butcher, and we looked over the field in front of us. Suddenly my comrade whispered;

'Henk, over there. A deer.'

As I looked in the direction he pointed out, I saw a deer walking over the field and scraping his hooves, to dig up some edible grass.

It was a beautiful animal but it was also ….food!

The butcher didn't think twice, aimed his rifle and shot.

The sound of the shot echoed over the field. Slowly the deer sunk through his legs and fell in the snow.

With a big cheer the butcher stood up and shouted; 'I nailed it. I nailed it'

We walked to the animal and as we approached I could see that it wasn't dead yet.

It looked at me. His big brown eye focused on me and for a moment

I felt sorry for that animal. Another casualty of the war, I thought.

The butcher took his pistol and finished the deer off. We dragged the animal back to our side of the field and the butcher started immediately to clean the deer and prepare it to eat.

Word spread around quickly in our unit that we killed a deer and many comrades came to try to get a part of it.

Because we didn't have any chairs to sit on, we used the dead and frozen Russian bodies as chairs.

Now, telling you this, it sounds so weird, but in that time, being numbed out of our emotions, nobody gave it a thought. It was 'normal'.

The deer was slowly roasted to perfection and everybody wanted a part of it.

When the butcher handed me my part of it, I refused.

Suddenly, as hungry as I was, I lost my appetite because I still had that image in my head of the deer looking at me with his big brown eye just seconds before he died.

I didn't even try to explain to my fellow comrades. They couldn't have understood it anyway.

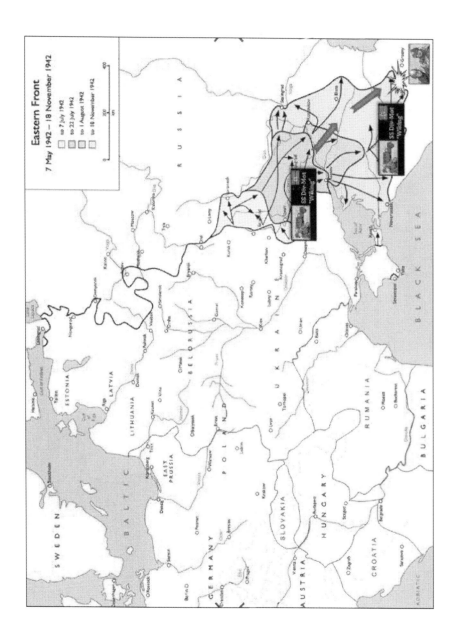

6

DIGGING AND VODKA

When we arrived in the village of Golubovka, somewhere in the Ukraine, it turned out to be 'Russian free' which was a Godsend situation for us. We had to dig a pit to put our mortar in but the soil was solidly frozen, and this proved to be a Herculean task.

Because of the severe cold the frontlines got mingled. It was not as simple anymore like 'they' are 'there' and 'we' are 'here'.

Because of the cold we didn't sleep out in the fields anymore but tried to make quarter in houses from the villagers.

Sometimes, with the frontlines mingled, you could get into a strange and dangerous situation.

My comrade Kruger and I were busy trying to shovel away the soil, but we hardly made any progress. Kruger, wiping the sweat off his forehead, sounded despondent when he said to me: "Henk, can you go to the nearest village and try to find us a pickaxe?"

I went back to the town of Golubovka and to my surprise, I found a civilian, a senior citizen, on the streets. I asked him for a pickaxe, but he had no clue what I was talking about.

So, I demonstrated how it looked when using a pickaxe and then he understood. A few moments later he brought me an axe. "Njet" I said, and made a drawing in the snow to explain what it was I was looking for. "Ah, Da, Da", (yes, yes) he responded and a few moments later he brought me what I was looking for. "Spassiba" (thanks) I answered him politely and went back to my mate Kruger.

It turned out that Kruger had got himself a spectator while I was gone.

The guy was dressed the same way as us, white clothing with a hoodie over his head.

"Let me help you", I told Kruger, and I jumped, with my pickaxe, into the pit.

Now we were working together and as we got deeper and deeper, the soil got softer and softer, and our job easier.

I was still hacking away, when I suddenly heard a shot, and to my amazement our spectator fell into our pit. Stupefied I looked at Kruger who held his still smoking gun in his hand.

"Man, what are you doing?", I stammered.

 Kruger looked appalled as he pointed at the dead man, (because he was as dead as a doornail) in our pit.

 "That guy was a Russian. I wanted to smoke a cigarette and asked him for a light, but he didn't react. As I asked again, he suddenly wanted to grab his machinegun which was hanging on his back. Luckily I turned out to react quicker than him."

I turned the body face upwards and now I saw it was somebody from 'the other side' as we called it. He smelled like he drank a whole bottle of Vodka and surely that may have been the reason he reacted too slow when it came to a 'it's a him or me' situation. He lost the most valuable of all, his life.

On February 22nd 1942, the Russians began another attack. They threw everything they had at us: infantry, artillery and tanks. After dark, their tanks made a circular move and now they were behind us. We kept up firing at their infantry in front of us and we heard them screaming and shouting. Probably they found courage at the bottom of a Vodka bottle again. Suddenly we got an artillery hit on the roof of the house that was our shelter. It started to burn, so we had to seek shelter somewhere else. I was the last one to leave the house and while doing that I saw to my left a bright white flash. I lost consciousness for a short time, then when I regained it, I heard somebody say:

"He has been hit also."

I was able to get up on my feet, but walked like I had also drunk a bottle of Vodka. Somebody told me where to find a doctor and I started swaggering that way. My guess was that I had been hit by shrapnel from one of their exploding tank rounds. I was still dizzy in my head and time and again I stumbled and fell into foxholes that I couldn't see in the dark.

Finally, I arrived at the doctor's post and the first thing they did was to give me a tetanus shot. Next, they started to ask me where I had sustained injuries. I couldn't tell because I felt no pain, only dazed.

At the end they put bandages around my knee, arm, neck and head.

Next move would be to transport me behind the lines. With all the other wounded soldiers that could be transported they put us on sleighs. The sleigh was packed with hay to make it more warm and comfortable.

During the night we moved through the line of Russian tanks. They couldn't see us, so we managed to get through without incident. We spent the rest of a night in an abandoned house in a nearby village to await the next day.

The following morning the sleigh convoy moved to, for me, an unknown destination.

Suddenly we were attacked by Russian 'Ratah's', (that's what we called their fighter planes).

The Russians didn't care if we had Red Cross banners on the sleighs, they attacked us anyway.

But as they always attacked in the flank, we got away unharmed.

Later we were transferred into a freight train to bring us to a field hospital where they could take really good care of us.

The first thing they did, after my arrival, was cut my uniform off from my body, and gave me a warm bath.

After that the surgeon investigated all of my wounds.

Every Waffen SS soldier has a tattoo with his SS number and blood type on his upper left arm.

It turned out that the shrapnel took so much flesh away, exactly on that spot, that there was no tattoo left anymore.

At the end of the war this would turn out to be very convenient.

They gave me a full anaesthetic before the operation and I regained consciousness again as they were putting me in bandages.

After that, they put me in a hospital room, and I could look around to check who was joining me there.

On my right side there was an Italian, who constantly moaned and repeated over, and over again the words "Oh mama mia".

He was shot in his stomach and in a very bad condition.

To my left side was a soldier from the Wehrmacht, whose whole body was packed in a cast of plaster.

Later they told me a grenade exploded right in front of his feet and it was a miracle the man was still alive to begin with.

In the right corner of the room, there was a guy who's behind was hit by a grenade and he constantly screamed; "It burns like hell. It burns like hell".

I guess, it would be very difficult for him to relax in a restroom over the coming weeks.

It took me almost four weeks, and periods with high fever, before I was ready to travel again.

When I was fever free they put me on a train.

A very comfortable passenger train, this time.

After a long ride, from which I spent most of the time sleeping, we stopped somewhere in Poland.

A soldier got onto the train and asked if anybody onboard the train was a member of the Waffen-SS.

I said "Yes" and had to leave the train immediately.

They brought me to the special Waffen-SS hospital in Krakau.

I stayed there, recovering for another 5 weeks.

After that they moved me to the town of Zakopane, near the Czech Republic border.

After two weeks, having a very comfortable stay over there, they put me on a train again, with two weeks leave to enjoy in my home country, the Netherlands.

Six days after I was wounded, on 28 February 1942, that day almost my whole battalion 'Germania' was destroyed and wiped out by the Russians.

From my company only 12 men and one NCO survived.

Almost all the members of my mortar squad died on the 28th of February, some died a couple of days later.

Getting wounded and transported far behind the front lines, turned out to be a blessing in disguise for me.

It was a strange, mixed feeling I had.

Of course, happy to have survived myself, but sad at the same time for losing all of my comrades.

7

CHOCOLATE

fter my return from the hospital and my short 'holiday' at home in the Netherlands, I was sent back to the Germania reserve battalion.

Before I was wounded, I was a member of the 4th company, but after the last battle, hardly any survivors were left, so they transferred me to the 1st company.

Needless to say, I didn't know anybody there.

I got assigned to the S.M.G section (Schweres Machinen Gewehr a.k.a Heavy Machine Gun or MG 34/42).

Originally I received training to be a part of an S.M.G group, but the time before I got wounded, I mostly served as a member of a mortar group.

Again, like when I was part of the 4th company, I was the only Dutchman in this whole group.

Then, the other day, war and its behaviour surprised me again. Just after my return, we took some Russian prisoners and some of them had German Shepherd dogs with them.

On the back of the dog, I noticed they had attached a package of explosives.

When I curiously asked what the purpose was of those explosives on the back of the dogs, they told me they used them against Germanski tanki (German Panzers).

Well, I wondered how you get a dog so crazy to crawl under a German panzer in order to be blown to smithereens?

The explanation was simple, they starved the dogs, until they became very hungry and then they conditioned the behaviour of the dog by feeding it, time and again, under a tank.

So now the dogs behaviour were so conditioned, that on the moment they saw a tank, they would release the dog with a burning fuse.

A so called unintentional suicide dog?

The dog would run straight under the tank, where he stayed, waiting for his food, until the explosives went off, killing the dog together with the tank.

Well, it looked like an ingenious plan, but we never experienced this in the field.

It turned out that the dogs preferred the Russian tanks (the ones they used to be trained with) above the German ones.

Who said dogs are stupid? No way!

They recognized their 'food' tanks and those were Russian! Karma!

In august of 1942, we were positioned at the Laba river and the temperatures were blistering hot.

We had to position our SMG close to the river, Our next SMG was just 50 meters to our right.

The Russians, at the other side of the river, expected our attack, but we had to regroup and reinforce our position, so for the time being everything was quite at the Eastern front.

We enjoyed our meal and lingered at the bank of the river.

Life wasn't that bad after all.

Suddenly, from our second SMG post, we heard a scream.

Somebody was hit, again (!) by a Russian sniper.

One of the guys from the other SMG came over to us and asked for bandages, because one of them had received a headshot.

A headshot? Well, even if he initially would survive this, I had bleak doubts about his future wellbeing.

The guy who caught the bullet, turned out to be a Belgian guy, a volunteer from the country just south of the Netherlands.

I knew him as a nice guy, but a little careless about his cover and that costed him dearly this time.

He didn't have much frontline experience and those guys (like me in the beginning) always thought they never would catch a bullet.

Yeah, right.

I went back with the soldier to the other SMG post, who asked us for the bandage, to see if I could be of any assistance.

The young Belgian soldier was bleeding like a slaughtered pig.

The bullet of the Russian sniper entered at his right cheekbone, just below his eye, went straight through the front part of his head and exited at the left side of his neck.

The shot went through his tongue, but probably missed his trachea, otherwise he would have been coughing up blood.

We took him out of harm's way and walked him to the medics.

He could walk normally, but talking was impossible for him.

After a 15 minute walk, we arrived at our medical care unit, where a nurse immediately took off the bandage of his neck and head. By doing this, the doctor could immediately see the damage and start treatment.

The doctor was still occupied with other surviving victims of the sniper.

So in the meanwhile, the nurse offered us a cup of chocolate milk, which I gladly accepted.

We hardly ever got this kind of treat, so this was an opportunity nobody would refuse.

Also the wounded Belgian guy accepted the chocolate milk and he poured it in his mouth, but with him it ran out through the hole in his neck!

Probably the bullet made a connection from his mouth to the side of his neck and that's where the chocolate milk ran out again.

His whole neck was colouring brown and it was an awkward sight to see, but it didn't seem to bother him at all. At least he managed to swallow most of it, I guess. Wonder how he did that anyhow?

I left the guy under the care of the medical team and went back to my unit.

I never saw him again after this incident, but even long after the war, when I drank chocolate milk, I had to think about this Belgian guy, somewhere at the banks of the river Laba in Russia.

Around Christmas 1942 we had to dig in.

To my surprise, they gave me a Russian POW to do the digging.

I wanted to hand him the shovel, so he could start his work, but he said: 'Nix Kuschait Pan?' (Nothing to eat, sir?)

Truthfully I told him, 'Njet nischto; (No, nothing)

His response was: 'Nix kuschait, Nix rabott' (No food, no work).

I was stunned, because, I would never ever say something like this, if I was to be a POW with the Russians. But he firmly refused to do any labour without being fed first.

He got balls, I had to give him that much credit.

At the end, I tried to dig the hole myself, but after a few futile attempts, I had to give up.

The soil was too hard.

As dinner was ready in our kitchen, it turned out to be chocolate rice.

We all loved that. We craved for everything that was sweet, because we hardly got that.

The Russian kids in those times often even didn't know what chocolate was?

I asked also an extra portion for my Russian POW.

Hopefully he would start digging after he got some food?

But when I came back to the spot where I left him, he was already gone?

I hoped he would be okay, because the Russians were not friendly at all to their returning POW's.

The good news? I got a double ration this day! Happiness always can be found in little things.

Later we had to move upwards, into the hills and, as we looked back to our old position, we saw around 20 Russian T-34 tanks driving in the same area we just had left.

There was no sign of any infantry troops to accompany those tanks.

As we went uphill, the tanks couldn't follow us, because it would be too steep for them.

But still, they could take a shot at us and I already looked for a suitable spot to hide, if they would start shooting their grenades at us.

As we carefully watched their movements, we noticed another 10 tanks, coming in from the left side.

Those tanks opened fire immediately, but not at us.

Their target turned out to be the group of 20 T-34's. To our joy and surprise those 10 tanks were German ones! From this distance, at first glance, we didn't recognize them.

Our joy became even bigger, as we saw, one after another, Russian T-34's being hit and burn.

This was mainly possible, because the Russian tanks made the big mistake in showing their flank too the oncoming German panzers.

If you are an experienced panzer commander and driver, you would always try to avoid showing your flank and/or backside of your panzer towards the enemy.

Those sides of a panzer have the least amount of protective armour. The front side of the panzer, is the side you engage to your enemy.

Because of this tactical mistake, only a few Russian T34's escaped the carnage and the rest were left ablaze on the battlefield.

The Tank crew that managed to get out, were mowed down by the machineguns of the German panzers. No survivors here.

We went on our way and after a while we could jump on the passing trucks that transported us to the city of Nalstjik. Here we made quarter and finally could enjoy a good night's sleep.

Note: The city of Nalstjik got international attention long after the war, when on 13 October 2005, an attack took place on a number of government buildings in the city, by armed fighters. The responsibility of which, was claimed by the Chechnyan terrorist, Shamil Basayev and at least 137 people got killed.

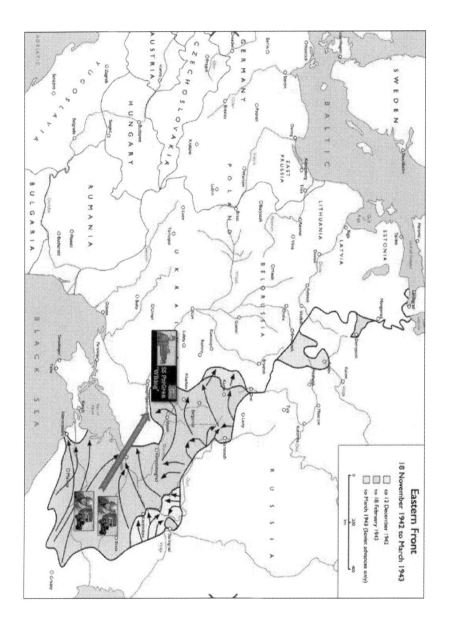

Eastern Front
18 November 1942 to March 1943

to 12 December 1942
to 18 February 1943
to March 1943 (Soviet advances only)

8

RECONNAISSANCE

n the first half of December 1942 our group, with exception of the ones with guard duties, were sitting in our bunker close to the heater.

Outside, luckily we still had no freezing temperatures, but it already was getting pretty chilly.

In the south of Russia, frost set in later than in the north part of this immense country.

Suddenly our commander came in: 'Boys', he said', we have to do a reconnaissance patrol tonight, because the other group has lack of manpower. So we have to help them out. Kistemaker and Hoffman are the volunteers for this night.'

I had to leave the relative safety and warmth of the bunker, but an order is an order.

I knew why he chose me though. At this moment I was already the guy with the longest time of service. Our whole battalion existed mainly of new recruits, hardly any experienced soldiers at all.

As a part of the SMG group, no one had any experience doing a reconnaissance patrol because normally this was a job for an infantry unit.

Of course, we also belonged to the infantry but to the platoon consisting heavy armor, like the SMG and mortars, and they didn't have to do reconnaissance. Until today, it seemed.

The army always could surprise you, time and again, by changing some habits or making exceptions to existing rules. You just had to go along with it. Swim with the flow, so to speak.

Hoffman was second in service time, that was the reason he too, became a 'volunteer'.

We had to report to the next bunker within 30 minutes and before we left, our commander provided us with a light machine gun instead of our regular pistol.

Hoffman and I reported for duty to the NCO at the other bunker.

He told us it would be our job to find out what kind of Russian unit was opposite our lines.

They told us it would be an elite unit, but to be sure we had to capture and bring back one or two of those Russian soldiers for interrogation. Easier said as done, in my opinion.

Well there are worse jobs than this, aren't there? Like clearing a minefield for example?

By the time we left it was 8 pm and pitch-dark.

Our group of six men went to the Russian frontlines and would try to catch us a couple of Russians.

It looked to me like a job description you don't want every day.

Besides this being an already a tricky task, we also had to be careful not to step on any mines.

I was second in line after our patrol leader and I watched very closely were he put his feet.

As long as he wasn't blown himself sky high, I could follow him. To be sure, I stepped exactly in his footprints but kept a safe distance.

Most of the time the mines were buried just under the top layer of the soil.

Walking very carefully doesn't help you a bit.

The moment you step on a mine, your weight will be enough and it will detonate right under your feet.

The Russians used mines in wooden boxes which were impossible to detect, even with a mine detector. No metal parts were used.

On top of the detonator they mounted a small, wooden board.

The moment you stepped on the wooden board, you pushed it downwards, the detonator would ignite the explosive charge and… boom….there you go! One way ticket to the hereafter or…if you were 'lucky', only missing one or two limbs.

The whole thing was not larger than a cigar box and the explosives looked like a clump of clay. The only way you could find them was by using a probe and carefully sticking it into the earth in front of you until you found one. If you found one you had to dig it up very, very carefully. I may sound scared shitless, but only a fool doesn't know fear, and will die very quickly.

My thoughts about the mines were the thoughts of all six of us.

Nobody spoke, but everybody's nerves were as tight as piano wire.

Slowly and carefully we moved forwards without any accidents or being detected.

Suddenly, the sound of a bang and a flare went up, lighting the sky in front of us.

Within a millisecond all six of us dropped flat to the ground and stayed still, not moving an inch.

My heart was bouncing in my throat and I was scared as hell.

But nothing happened. The flare died out slowly, high up in the sky, and after a while we felt it was safe enough to get up and continue our way.

I remembered that we did, in our lines, the same thing as the Russians did just now.

Just occasionally shoot a flare over the frontlines in front of you, to check if you could detect any enemy movements.

We continued our way, which led us slowly downhill.

(Most of the time if we had the chance, we would build our lines on higher ground. It gave you a tactical advantage over the enemy.)

The platoon leader stopped and made a hissing sound.

He saw something. He had night vision binoculars and scanned the area around us. As far as the night vision binoculars, they were introduced into the German army before the start of World War Two.

No one moved or spoke for the short time that he looked. He turned around and made it clear to us that 40 or 50 meters straight ahead of us, he detected a Russian guard.

Probably the guy hadn't heard us coming because he didn't move. He just stood there.

When we had guard duty at night we closed our eyes to improve our hearing. That actually helps.

In the dark you had no use of your eyes so by closing them, your ears started to work more intensively.

The platoon leader chose Hoffman and me to go with him (again).

The others had to provide us with coverage from the right and the left side.

Shots were only allowed to be fired in an utter case of emergency, because it would wake up the whole frontline and that party you really don't want to attend.

With bouncing hearts we crawled to our destination, because at this time it was too dangerous to walk standing straight up.

While doing this it popped up in my mind that I hadn't had one more thought about the mines.

My mind was already preoccupied with one dangerous task, so I totally forgot about the other.

When we were close to the Russian guard, we made a circular movement to the right so we ended up behind him.

Now we took a short break to catch our breath, because crawling takes a lot of energy, I can tell you that.

In a whispered tone, we communicated about how we would deal with this situation.

At this moment all my nervousness and fear was gone. I was calm and in complete control of myself. The platoon leader decided he would creep up to the guard and once behind him, he would stand up straight, put the machine gun in his back and tell him; 'Ruki Werch'(Hands up). Meanwhile, we would approach the guard from the left and right side and disarm him after our leader had him under his control. Don't they say life is happening to you while you're busy planning it? Well, that turned out to be exactly what would happen here.

We still had about 20 meters to go when we discovered a sort of a bulge in the earth .

After careful examination it turned out to be a Russian bunker. The other members of the Russian group were, for sure, sleeping in there.

Now what? Change of plans. Our platoon leader made the decision: 'Kistemaker, you come along with me. Hoffman, you stay at the entrance of that bunker. In case of any danger, open that door and throw a couple of hand grenades in there.'

Now my heart was pounding like crazy again.

'Shit, what kind of situation I got myself into again?'

But no time for worrying. We moved slowly forwards until we were close to the guard.

He still didn't hear anything coming to him. Must be deaf or we were that good.

At a signal from my platoon leader, we both leapt forwards and grabbed the guard.

The man gave a scream from anxiety and Hoffman, who thought this could turn into a dangerous situation quickly opened the door to the bunker, threw two hand grenades inside and closed the door again. This was an alarm bell from which you never would wake up again.

After the two hand grenades exploded in the bunker, nobody came out. But to our left and our right, flares went up into the sky. Now all hell was about to break loose.

Our Russian guard tried to use this moment for an escape attempt, but my platoon leader raised his MP and shot a couple of bullets into him. The Russian collapsed to the ground, probably dead and therefore useless for interrogation. Shit, now we had nobody to take back to our lines.

Crawling, we left the Russian lines on our way back to our lines.

The other three men of our group whom we had left behind knew already something went terribly wrong. By the sound of their voices we managed to orientate ourselves and crawled back to them.

Once we reached them we rested for a while, because meanwhile the whole frontline was wide awake and everybody started shooting at everybody.

Bullets and flares, but nothing was really aimed at anybody or anything.

It was just a panic shooting.

After everything settled down again we had to try to get back to our own lines.

Our mission had failed. We didn't bring a Russian prisoner back for interrogation. Well, shit happens.

Most imported thing for us was getting back alive and in one piece, if possible.

After a while, what seemed like hours to us, a German guard heard something out there in the field in front of him and asked for the password.

Of course, they knew that out there would be a reconnaissance unit. But everybody approaching our lines from the 'wrong side' had to be called upon and present a password.

Once back, we had a great story to tell to everybody who stayed behind.

It didn't take a genius to figure out this mission didn't go like planned, but at least we survived.

It turned out that this was my first, last and only night reconnaissance for the rest of the war.

I can't say I will miss it.

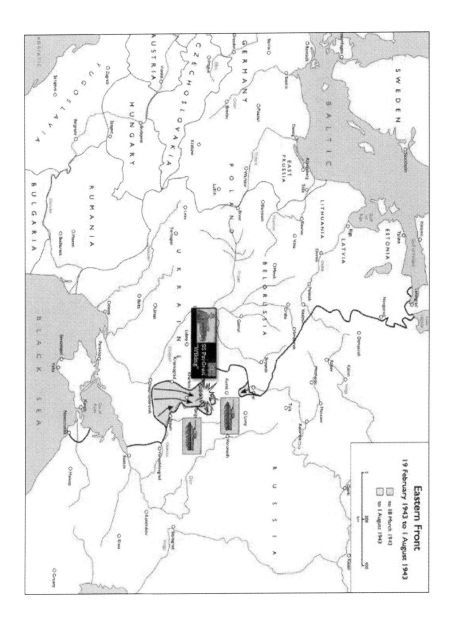

9

HOFFMAN AND JAHN

On January 17th 1943 we left the village where we had our last quarters.

None of the transport vehicles could make it through the snowy fields and this meant we had to walk carrying all of our equipment.

Although it started snowing and there was a heavy wind blowing, I was comfortable.

The reason for that was because of the first time ever they provided us, with actual winter clothing.

We thought that headquarters expected we would stay here at least another winter, maybe even two?

I wore a field cap over my head instead of a helmet. In fact, nobody wore his steel helmet anymore, because the metal conducted the cold.

Oddly enough, I felt safe and comfortable within my winter clothing, like the warmth protected me from the war and the cold and therefore nothing could happen to me.

I think, people built on little securities to keep sane. If you lived in constant fear, you wouldn't be able to function anymore.

Shortly before we went into battle, fear and anxiety always kicked in with me, but the moment the fighting actually started, I always felt calm and in control.

We came to another village and the order came to put our machine gun in position near the first house of the village.

Next to the house we noticed somebody had already dug a foxhole.

That was nice, it saved us a lot of digging.

We only had to expand it a little bit and after this, we had a pretty good position.

A machine gun crew consist of 5 members. Everybody had a specified task, from the gunner, the ammo bearer (man who had to keep the ammunition in stock). The ammo bearer was always running to and fro, from our ammo depot, just behind the frontlines. Because he was the last one in the line of this, they called him 'Schutze Arsch' (Gunner Ass)

About 100 meters to our right, we could see a semidetached building.

It was hardly visible, because the snow storm was still blowing.

The three of us (Hoffman, Jahn and myself) decided to check it out.

The other two crew members stayed in our foxhole.

Hoffman decided to take a light MG along (you never know), I was second and behind me, Jahn, closed the line.

Walking through the blizzard of snow, we kept our heads down to avoid the blowing snow, meanwhile we tried to maintain a casual conversation with each other.

Suddenly Hoffman stopped in front of me, and I almost bumped into him.

We looked at him and he said: 'Silence, I hear something'

Now all three of us started to listen, to see if we could pick up any of the sounds Hoffman claimed to have heard. And yes, indeed, behind the targeted building, we could hear hammering.

Steel onto steel, or so it sounded.

Very cautious, we closed in on the building.

In fact, that was over the top cautious, because the snowstorm made so much noise that nobody would hear us coming anyway, but at the moment we were all a little bit nervous.

And it is as they say: better safe than sorry.

Hoffman was the first of us, who reached the corner of what turned out to be a big barn.

Carefully, he looked around the corner and pulled his head back immediately, whispering: 'T-34'

Now we want to see it for ourselves and he was right (like he could be wrong, but we wanted to see it for ourselves anyhow).

It was a T-34, parked at the side of the barn and the rear of the tank faced us.

On top, at the rear of the tank, a crew member was doing something but we had no clue what Meanwhile, two other crewmen were hammering on a part of the tracks from the tank.

It looked, to us, like they had a broken track and they were trying to fix it.

This was the sound Hoffman had heard and got his attention, the metal on metal hammering..

The fourth crew member was nowhere to be seen (Russian T-34's have 4 crew members).

We assumed he was still inside the tank? This assumption would cost us dearly.

We pulled back and started to deliberate, how we would deal with this situation?

Hoffman said; 'I still have a Molotov cocktail in my backpack. Can you take it out Henk?'

I opened his backpack and felt with my hands, until I found what I was looking for: the Molotov cocktail bottle.

This bottle, we had captured it from the Russians previously.

Unfortunately the German army didn't have anything like this, because sometimes it could be pretty useful. Like right now, for example.

Note: A Molotov cocktail is a breakable glass bottle containing a flammable substance such as gasoline, alcohol or a napalm-like mixture, with some motor oil added, and usually a source of ignition such as a burning cloth wick held in place by the bottle's stopper. The wick is usually soaked in alcohol or kerosene, rather than petrol.

In action, the wick is lit and the bottle hurled at a target such as a vehicle or fortification. When the bottle smashes on impact, the ensuing cloud of fuel droplets and vapor is ignited by the attached wick, causing an immediate fireball followed by spreading flames as the remainder of the fuel is consumed.

I wanted to hand over the bottle to Hoffman, but he said: 'No , Henk, I will keep them covered with the MG and you can throw the bottle, because you can throw the farthest of all three of us.'

That made no sense at all, because the T-34 was not even 10 meters away from us, but I accepted the challenge.

Shaking all over my body from nervousness, I was lying there holding the Molotov cocktail, hoping I could make the perfect throw. The outcome of this action would depend on my performance. I felt a heavy responsibility on my shoulders now.

Hoffman, tired of me stalling my throw, said : 'Henk, are you ready, or what? I am ready to shoot.' With a deep sigh, I got up, until I was on my knees, bended a little backwards and made my throw in the direction of the T-34.

Immediately, I ducked away for cover. At that moment I heard the rattling of our MG and at the T-34, somebody screamed.

As I looked around the corner and saw the T-34 burning (it was a perfect throw) and three crew members, lying on the ground. The man, who just had been standing on the rear of the tank, was now burning from head to toe. To my left side, I saw Hoffman and Jahn also coming out of their cover.

But suddenly somebody started shooting at us.

I felt an incredible hard punch against my right lower leg and I saw Hoffman and Jahn being shot and tumbling dead onto the snowy ground.

In a reflex, I pulled my handgun and shot a couple of times in the direction, where the shots came from.

There I saw a figure and after my shots, he dropped his rifle and ran away.

Probably, I hit his hand or his gun, with my poorly aimed shots, but it saved my life.

Now the pain kicked in. I was unable to stand up. It turned out I had, what the Germans called, 'ein durchschuss' or a 'through and through' shot in my right leg.

Probably only a flesh wound, but man, did it hurt.

I was wriggling in the snow from the pain, afraid that any moment the 4th crew member of the T-34 would come back to finish what he had started.

I heard our other crewmembers calling for us. At the top of my lungs, I shouted back, still afraid the Russian tank crew man would return.

After a short while, our commander was the first to arrive on the scene.

'What the hell happened here?', he said, as he looked at my two dead comrades and at me.

He couldn't see the T-34, because it was burning behind the barn.

Painfully, I explained what had happened. Now he really started to be pissed off: 'Why did you act on your own? We are already shorthanded and because of this I now have an incomplete machine gun crew!'

He was right, but it was all water under the bridge now. We couldn't turn back the clock.

My comrades fetched a sleigh from somewhere, put me on it and dragged me back to our foxhole. There I had to wait, until the ambulance picked me up and transported me to a hospital (again).

During my trip the pain in my leg got less, it now felt more like a kind of numbness.

I was more in a mental pain, because of the loss of my two friends, now buried somewhere in the Ukraine.

But there was nothing that could change the fact they were dead and I was alive.

In the hospital the doctor came to me, looked at my leg, made a whizzing sound as he pointed with his finger from the left to the right. Insiders knew, he meant; 'The shot went through your leg?' I nodded and he went away.

That same night, they transported me again with an ambulance, to the train station. The train was packed with wounded soldiers, who had just been flown in from Stalingrad.

They were probably the last batch of lucky bastards who made it out alive, as history would show us.

Because it was a freight train, we could sit on a thick layer of hay, so I didn't mind.

They transported us to the hospital of Artimovsk, a city in the Ukraine.

After I received new bandages, the doctors started to make selections for those going back to Germany.

They had to clear out the hospital. Around this time we were losing some territory to the Russians. And the Russians would shoot every wounded soldier in the hospital. That happened already before. No mercy for the wounded.

Because I couldn't walk, they transported me immediately back to a train and off I went.

Our train journey took a long time. It went on and on and on and nobody had a clue where we were going?

Finally we arrived in a very big city and that turned out to be Vienna in Austria. Back into civilization.

They laid me down on a stretcher in the hallway. I was wearing only a short shirt, for the rest I was naked.

It was a little awkward to be so exposed with everybody, nurses and doctors, walking through that hallway.

After a while two nurses came to pick me up, but before any bandaging would be done, they first gave me a bath. Not an unnecessary treatment, I can tell you that as most of the time we were covered with lice.

After this, they placed me in a room with two other patients.

One of them was a guy from Vienna.

He was lucky, because his wife regularly visited him and brought him a toothbrush and other paraphernalia.

I had nothing, absolutely nothing.

Because I was bedridden I had to use a bedpan. I didn't like to use a bedpan.

As soon as I felt the urge to go, I managed to drag myself out of bed and limped my way to the restrooms.

But halfway, I lost my balance and I would have made a hard fall on the stone floor, if it wasn't for a nurse, who prevented me from actually falling.

She was pissed off because I left my bed and reprimanded me, but also gave me an apple. A fruit, I had not had for a very long time.

After six weeks in Vienna, I was able to walk, well more limp, through the hospital and I volunteered to be discharged from the hospital.

They agreed with that and already the next morning, I found myself on a train to Amsterdam, my birthplace, in the Netherlands.

I was accompanied by another German soldier, whose hometown was the city of Munich.

So during the first part of the journey we traveled together.

After I spent about 10 days at my parents' house, I got a telegram that said; 'Abort your furlough. Leave immediately for Klagenfurt, Austria.'

Saying goodbye is never easy, but surely not for a mother who lived day in and day out in fear that she would receive a message from the German army, that would say; 'Your son has fallen for the honor of the Third Reich blah, blah, and so on '

When I arrived in Klagenfurt, I met I guy, who likerwise, came back from 'wounded furlough'.

He got a bullet through the lower part of his arm in the area of Malgobek.

I knew that area well, we lost a lot of man over there.

Like me, he was lucky to have survived.

Although his arm was still a little bit stiff, they declared him 'kriegsverwendungsfahig' or ready to serve in the war again.

From Klagenfurt in Austria, they transported us to Prague capitol of the Czech Republic, just to transit to Debica, which is about 100 km from Kremsier in the Chech Republic.

In Debica, the military training facility turned out to be almost completely empty, so we could chose which room and bed we wanted.

We had nothing to do there, except wandering around, sleep and eat.

It was a boring and a gloomy place to be, so we were happy when they put us on a train again.

This journey ended in Grafenwohr, in the southern part of Germany.

Here was a big training facility and I ended up bunking in a room filled with all Danish guys.

They taught me a couple of Danish sentences and words, that I can still remember.

They put me through machine gun training again. Probably they thought I wouldn't know how to shoot after my leg wound?

On the shooting range I nailed it with 59 out of 60 shots. you had to shoot on a board, that was divided in six areas. It was perfect if you had 10 hits in every area.

I had 10 hits in five of the six areas, so this was nearly perfect.

One day, during my stay in Grafenwohr, we got a visit from our beloved General Felix Steiner. We all loved and respected Felix Steiner and suddenly, while standing in line, he stopped right in front of me and asked me my rank and name.

After hearing my name he said; 'You are Dutch, aren't you?'

After I confirmed I was Dutch he started to ask me where I had been and what experiences I had.

After hearing my stories, he called the commander and said; 'This man should be immediately awarded the Iron Cross second class.' I was also awarded with '*das verwundetenabzeichen*' (medal for having been wounded 3 times or more) and the 'frozen meat' winter war award, for surviving the winter of '41-'42. Steiner also said he wanted me to be promoted to be an NCO.'

After this avalanche of compliments, he asked me if I had, maybe a wish?

'Yes sir', I told him, 'I would love to be a crew member of the newly formed Panther battalion.'

He approved my request and I went into training.

Because of my school education in the Netherlands, as a radio-operator, they assigned me as the machine gunner/radio-operator.

That is in the right front side of the Panther panzer. I would spent the rest of the war in this position.

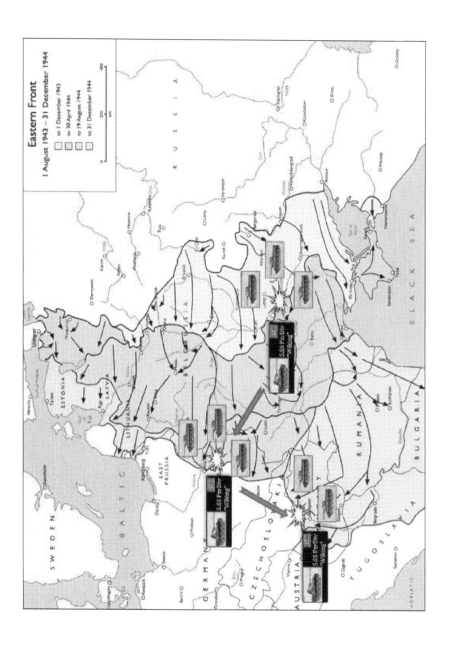

10

INFORMATION

f I talk about panzers I always talk about "The Panzer" I was allowed to drive within.

It is quite deliberately I say 'allowed', because I considered it to be a great privilege.

After me being reassigned to the panzer division, I first had to undertake the NCO training and after this was completed, they shipped us to Sankt Valentin in Austria.

During the Second World War the Nibelungen factory was located in Sankt Valentin; the second largest panzer factory in Nazi Germany.

Here, along with other panzers, the Tiger I was built.

We had to help in assembling in building and assembly of the Panzer 4, this was to get ourselves acquainted with panzers as a machine and as a weapon.

This only lasted two weeks, but during this short period I met my future wife to be.

She came from the city of Wurzburg, Germany and was on a holiday in this area while I was stationed there.

After this we became pen pals until we married in 1953. But that's a different story.

For our next level of training, we were transported to Erlangen.

Erlangen is located in the north-west of Nuremberg, Bavaria.

Here we got acquainted with the new Panzer V, or the so-called

Panther. (Panzer MK4 chassis with thicker frontal armor a better Engine and a bigger Canon)

Then, after a short while, we were transferred, this time to Mailly-le-Camp, a small commune in north-central France. (160km East of Paris)

Here we actually got to drive and operate the Panther and also had shooting practice.

After the completion of this training and receiving the beautiful, black panzer uniform, we were ready to be put back into action.

Suddenly we got orders to get shipped immediately, to the eastern part of Poland.

We were transported without any panzers, they were to follow with on a different transport at a later time.

Our journey ended in the Polish city Chelm, only 90 kilometers away from Kovel a town in the northwest part of the Ukraine.

Kovel was surrounded by the Russian army and they occupied parts of the city at this time.

In March and April 1944, Kovel would be the site of fierce fighting between our 5th SS Panzer Division Wiking and the Red Army.

Our new Panthers arrived shortly after our arrival.

Every company got 17 panzers. A (typical) company was divided into 3 platoons.

Every platoon consisted of 5 panzers.

On top of that, 2 panzers were assigned: one for the company commander and one for the troop leader. In total the whole division had 79 panzers.

Being the 'funker' (radio-operator) this had its benefits.

The radio-operator, together with the driver, had the best seats in the panzer, and, for me, also the safest place.

Our spot, in the front part of the panzer, they called 'Die Wanne' or 'The Tub' . As for the other 3 crewmembers, they were 'In die Turm' or 'the turret'.

Often when I caught up with my old friends in the Infantry, they asked me:

'Henk, why in the hell did you volunteer to be placed in that steel coffin?'

Most infantry men were too scared to sit in a panzer.

If the enemy would start shooting at you, and believe me they WILL, you have nowhere to go, nowhere to hide, just wait if and hope you would get through it. You need to have nerves of steel.

One time, later in the war, when our Luftwaffe (Airforce personnel) almost had no planes left to fly, they would put a pilot as a crewmember into our panzer. Because our loader fell ill (yeah, actually normally ill, that happened also, you know), we got this pilot as a replacement, but after ONE battle, they had to take him to a mental hospital with a nervous breakdown. This guy, because he was used flying high in the sky and free as a bird, couldn't stand the claustrophobic environment that a panzer will give you.

On top of that, everybody from the enemy side wants you dead, nothing personal, but still. Being inside the panzer, with all those impacts and the hammering of bullets and shrapnel against the hull and glowing metal particles, flying around everywhere, it broke him mentally in only one battle. We never saw him again. Totally emotionally destroyed, that guy.

Infantry men also were free to seek cover everywhere they could.

It gave them that false sense of security of having control of their lives. And hope is what keeps us all alive, isn't it?

I will tell you now about the crew of the Panther.

In the turret you have 3 crewmembers, the commander, the loader and the gunner.

From those 3, the loader had the most space, but no seat.

He had to be able, to maneuver the big shells from the magazine to the canon.

Behind him was a hatch to get in and out and also for loading, or unloading, the rounds and other things we needed to store or had to dispose of in or out of the panzer.

The gunner had the worst place of all, he had a small seat and the legs of his commander were hanging over his shoulders.

To get out of the panzer, he had to wait until the commander had got out first.

Certainly, not a position to envy, especially in a case of emergency, like if the fuel tanks getting hit and the panzer was catching on fire.

Or if the commander was wounded or even worse, dead. He would be trapped like a mouse in a cage.

The commander had no seat, only a stool, no backrest available.

The turret was able to circle a complete 360 degrees.

This could be done by hand (slow) or with an electro engine, operated by a foot pedal of the gunner. Most of the time, it was a combination of the two: A quick turn to get the gun in the general direction of the target and fine tuning by hand to lock it precisely on the target.

In the 'tub' you had the best seats of the panzer, seats with backrests and with a sort of shock absorber, because driving with a panzer in those days, was not a pleasant Sunday cruise.

The driver had the control of the 740 HP V12 engine, with 10 gears. 7 forwards and 3 backwards, as far as I recall. The Panther was not able, like the lighter panzers, to turn on the spot.

The lighter panzers were able to let one track going backwards and the other going forwards.

Because of this, they could turn in a small, circular movement.

We also couldn't, like the lighter panzers, stand on top of a foxhole and wiggle to and fro, to crush any enemy hiding in there.

The driver of the Panther had two handles, one for the left track and one for the right.

He could only let one track go slower than the other one, but NOT going with one track in the opposite direction.

We had a starting engine, to start the panzer, but to save the battery life, we used a handle to manually turn the flywheel, outside at the back of the panzer.

That job was assigned to the loader and the radio-operator.

It was heavy work and mainly done in winter time, because the cold affected the performance of our batteries.

The Russian T34 had, only on that point at least, an advantage to the Panther.

They could start their tank with the help of a built in pressure tank of compressed air, that would refill immediately after the engine had started.

But turning their turret had to be done completely manually. This was a major disadvantage during battle, in my opinion.

In the turret the commander could see the landscape laid out like the digits of a clock from 1 to 12.

Digit 12 means 'straight ahead' Digit 3 means 'to the right' Digit 9 'to the left' Digit 6 'Straight to the back' And so on.

On board, we had 2 kinds of rounds.

To eliminate an enemy tank, we used anti-tank rounds, recognizable by a black tip.

Against infantry and PAK (Panzer Abwehr Kanone or anti-tank guns) we used explosive rounds.

It worked as follows.

The commander spotted, for example, an enemy tank, most of the time a T-34, and he would give the order by the, on board, radio communication: 'Enemy tank on 2 o'clock'.

The gunner would use his foot pedal to swing the turret into that direction, fine-tune it by hand, until the arrow in his optics would stand between the digits 1 and 2.

He then would say: 'Ziel erkannt'(Target recognized).

Also the distance to the target needed to be mentioned, but only if the target was further away than 800 meters and lower than 2 meters in height.

In all other cases, the gunner would, if he had aimed correctly in the first place, always hit the target. The Panther was able to knock out a T-34 from a distance of 2000 meters.

From the other side: the T-34 had to get as close as 800 to 1000 meters to our panzer to be able to knock us out.

Because of this we obviously had, a tactical advantage on the enemy. The problem was, there were so many T-34's. The re-produced like rabbits. Kill 100 of them, next day you would see another 100.

In real combat, this whole routine would go much faster.

The loader automatically handed the gunner an anti-tank round, the moment he heard 'Enemy tank sighted' or he grabbed already a High Explosive Shell if he heard 'Infantry or PAK sighted!'.

Also the gunner did not need to wait on the commander to shout 'fire' if he got his target in his sights.

I also did not need a command to 'fire' if our tank encountered enemy infantry. I would just open fire. Only if I hadn't seen them (my vision was less than the commander at that spot) the commander would give the direction and the order to shoot.

The gunner, the radio-operator and the commander all had an MG34 at their disposal.

Also we had to stand still to make a good shot. If you see these movies from WW2 with tanks blasting their guns, while driving: it's nonsense.

You would probably hit another planet in our solar system quicker, than an enemy tank.

Why? In those days, the turret was not independently moving from the chassis/body.

So if our panzer tilted downwards, the turret would go along.

If you would drive in rough terrain (where a tank most of the time has his playground) you are in for a bumpy ride.

Therefore, while driving, you could NEVER successfully aim on a target.

You had to stop in order to do so accurately.

These days tanks are equipped with a gun stabilizer. A device intended to facilitate aiming a gun by compensating for the motion of the platform on which the gun is mounted, to be short: whatever movement the undercarriage would make, the turret stays always on the level.

This allows the tank to move and shoot accurately at the same time and increases the survivability on the battlefield.

Well, we didn't have that. So, we had to stop, before we could shoot accurately.

The radio-operator had his radio equipment to his left side

From this spot, I couldn't see the driver because of all the radio equipment in between us, only if I leaned backwards.

I controlled the internal communication of the panzer, but being in the panzer of the company commander, I also maintained communication with other panzers, and also with HQ (Headquarters).

Behind my chair and behind the driver's seat, there was a stack of rounds.

All the other rounds were in the vicinity of the loader, which is logical of course,

On average we would carry around 80 rounds with us.

The loader was the only one without a headset, because it would limit his movements too much. He only could listen to the commanders orders.

Visibility in a panzer, let's be clear about this, it's poor if not terribly poor.

The commander had the best view out of all of us, but he also had the greatest risk of being hit by a sniper.

This happened, in the last months of the war, to my friend Hans Heufler.

He got a headshot, after which his panzer got hit by an anti-tank grenade and burnt out completely, together with the whole crew.

The Russians looked for an opportunity like this to take out the commander.

They knew with a dead commander, the panzer was as good as useless.

The gunner could only see through his optics.

The loader had a periscope optic, that enabled him to look only to the left side.

He also could open the hatch in the back side of the turret, but this was, needless to say, strictly forbidden during an enemy engagement.

The driver also had a periscope optic, with a fixed view to the left, but he also had a small hatch in front of him. If opened, the opening would be still protected by thick armored glass.

Also the glass could be removed from the inside, but, again, this was strictly forbidden during battle time.

I will tell you a story about neglecting that advice and the consequences of it in one of my next stories.

Most of the times people get killed, by not obeying the (safety) rules or by some other stupid mistake.

Also my view, of the radio operator, machine gunner, was very limited.

I had a non-movable optic, with vision to the right and I had my machine gun optics.

The machinegun was mounted in a movable ball of steel and therefore, after the commander, I had the 'best' view.

Sometimes we had to transport wounded men.

If only one, we could put him in together with the loader, because there was space for one wounded soldier.

Sometimes we would get hitchhikers.

Infantry men, they would like to ride on the back of the panzer, the engine area, if we were on our way for an attack.

They thought, they would be safe, riding on the back of that enormous scary panzer.

Well, let me tell you: nothing is less true than this.

Every veteran, with enough combat experience, keeps a big distance between him and their panzers. Only unexperienced rookies would climb on the back of it.

The reason for this is simple.

The moment the German panzer appeared on the battlefield and got noticed by the Russians, everybody, and I mean E-V-E-R-Y-B-O-D-Y, started to shoot at that panzer, with every weapon they could find.

Bullets, hand grenades, bombs, artillery, you name it and they threw it at you.

Needless to say that, if you thought you were having a snug ride on the back of that panzer, you would be human mash potato in a short matter of time.

During battle time it was also forbidden for the panzer crew to leave the panzer. Just to avoid unnecessary losses of course.

If one crew member gets injured or killed during his 'time out of the panzer', it would paralyze the operational quality of that whole panzer.

It seems like such a minor thing, but human needs also keep on going, also during battle time.

Often just CAUSED BY the battle time. And remember there is NO toilet in the panzer, forget it.

If you had to defecate during battle, and believe me that regularly happened, you couldn't just say; 'Can you park over there? I will be back in 5 minutes.'

The solution? We took the shells of the used rounds and defecated inside them.

Needless to say that the smell of shit, combined with human sweat and gunpowder from the fired rounds, didn't make the inside of a panzer smell like roses. As soon as there was an opportunity, we quickly would dispose of all those 'smelly' shells.

Besides the two kind of rounds, I told you about previously, we also had, so called, smoke grenades on board.

If we had to leave the panzer in an emergency, if he had time, the commander would throw the smoke grenades, almost immediately obscuring the panzer in a covering fog (Smokey) cloud.

This made escaping a little bit less tricky, because(however) a random bullet could (still) get you anyway.

We also used the smoke grenades, if we wanted to pull back unseen with our panzer.

Hidden under the cover of a fog cloud, allowed us to turn around and retreat quickly.

The worst enemy of a panzer is not, as you might think, another enemy tank.

No, it's the PAK or a stand of PAK's (Panzer Abwehr Kanone or Anti-Tank gun).

They were more difficult to spot than an enemy tank.

Often hiding behind a slope or in bushes or on the edge of a forest.

Very difficult for is to see and most often, very well camouflaged.

Shots from those guns came, most of the time, as a complete surprise to us.

Destroying a PAK gave you the same credits, as destroying another enemy tank.

We HATED them and if we had a chance to take them out, we would do so, and sometimes afterwards, we would drive over the PAK stands, crushing, with our 45 tons of steel, both the men and machine that would still be there.

One time, after a battle, I took a look reviewing what was left and I saw, guns, horses and human bodies completely crushed.

Their heads and bodies were totally flat. It looked disgusting and awful but, hey, that's war.

Note from Peter: As I visited the Bovington tank museum, somewhere in the first decade of the new century, the curator let me climb on one of the Panthers in their showroom. My father told me, that they managed to be up, on and in control of their Panther within a minute, due to their excessive training.

I tried to squeeze myself into his spot, the radio operator, by the hatch above 'his' head and with difficulty managed to maneuver myself in.

Also the hatch for the loader, although with better access, gave me trouble, bumping my head everywhere and I really started to feel respect for the crew of those Panthers, being able to live and fight there with a crew of five and doing their job.

Military historians still debate about which was the best tank of the Second World War, but for all the polls and spec comparisons, the Panzer V Panther is always one of the contenders at the top. Given its speed and off-road capabilities, tremendous firepower, protection, sophisticated targeting sights, use of equipment far ahead of its time (like infrared vision) and, last but not least, the fact that more than 6000 machines that were built, the Panther could maybe potentially have turned the outcome of the war if Germany ONLY would have decided to have built this version of the tanks, instead of all those other types they built.

Being one of the best-balanced designs of WWII, it performed accordingly, with a fear capital, almost rivalling that of the Tiger.

For my father the answer was obvious: The Panther was the best tank of WW2, according to him. Only outperformed by the T-34 NOT in quality, but only by numbers, he said.

Okay, he was biased, but still….he got a point there.

11
MACIEJOV

Around **April 1944, Kovel In the Ukraine, had** been surrounded by the Russians: Most parts of the city had already been occupied.

In the city itself, there were many German nurses cut off from the German lines, their futures didn't look too bright should the Russians get a hold of them.

Later, when the Russians actually invaded the German homelands, brutal things happened to many of the women from the German villages and cities.

Many were raped, sometimes by dozens of soldiers, others were mutilated and I heard stories from people in Berlin, that they actually cut off the breasts of women after they raped them and then left them to die.

No, we knew already that in the hands of the Russians, they wouldn't make it, so high command decided to get these poor women out of Kovel, before this doom scenario could unfold.

On April 5th 1944, the company commander of the 8th company, 2nd battalion, Karl Nicolussi-Leck, (we shortcut his name to Nico) from Austria, opened the attack on Kovel.

The problem was the marshland around the whole city. This made it Impossible for the Panzers to drive through.

Because of their weight (45 tons) they would become bogged down and wouldn't be able to get out again.

The only way to get into the city would be to drive over the railroad embankment .The disadvantage of this, was that the Panzers would have to drive one after another, and while doing so would be an easy target for the anti-tank guns.

If, for instance, the first panzer was knocked out, then the others wouldn't be able to move forward anymore.

All in all very risky, but the only available option at that time.

Nico managed to break through the encirclement and got into the city, only to find out that the encirclement had closed round behind him! Now it was up to us to get him out.

The next day, April 6th 1944, the 5th, 6th and 7th Panzer divisions from Wiking were to start the attack on Kovel.

Our division, the 6th, started the attack from the north-east together with the 4th Panzer division of the Wehrmacht (regular German army).

Our freedom of movement was also limited because of the marshlands, so we used the embankment of the railroad.

It was very dangerous and difficult, but we made progress.

We took the village of Kruhel and afterwards , the village Dubove.

Finally we entered Kovel from the north side of the city.

By this time, the Russians were all over the city and even in our area, they occupied some streets.

Urban battles are disliked by any tank crew.

Tanks don't like to fight in areas that are unclear, like forest or urban areas.

Especially urban areas which are a nightmare. In every building, every house you might have Russians with Nahkampfmittel, or so called close combat weapons, like hand grenades, Molotov cocktails or panzerfausts (bazooka).

Around every corner, there might be a PAK stand, so this was a really precarious operation.

On the first day of that urban fight, we had already lost our first panzer!

It turned out to be the 633, those numbers meaning, 6th company, 3rd battalion, 3rd panzer.

What happened?

Well, I told you earlier that many times accidents and deadly accidents occurred because people disobeyed safety regulations, this was one of those occasions.

The driver of the 633 was a Dutch guy, from the city of Woerden, Dick van Vliet.

He was a nice guy, but didn't follow the safety procedures this day. That would cost him and almost all of his crewmembers their lives.

The 633 was attacked by Russian infantry, who had tried to take out the panzer with hand grenades.

An impossible task, if all the hatches had been closed, but…they still tried. You couldn't say the Russians lacked persistence.

Dick van Vliet opened the hatch in front of him, took out the 10cm thick, bullet proof glass (STRICTLY forbidden during combat!), grabbed his pistol and started shooting at those infantry men.

At the same time, 200 meters In front of him, a Russian PAK, calibre 3.7 cm took a shot at the 633. Normally a 3.7 cm grenade wouldn't penetrate the thick armour of the Panzer, but with pure bad luck, the grenade went directly through the opened hatch in the front of the tank, ripping off the head of Dick van Vliet, and exploding in the ammunition behind him.

As a result of the whole panzer exploded.

The only person who came out alive was the commander, whose name was Dimmer.

He passed our panzer in the back of a truck, calling my name, I recognized his voice.

His face was totally burned and was swollen up like a balloon. End of the war for this guy, but at least he survived.

After the battle and when the destroyed panzer had cooled down enough, we had to clean the burned out 633 of human remains.

The only thing I found of Dick van Vliet, was a completely charred femur bone. Nothing more.

A burning panzer can develop more than 1000 degrees Celsius, so inside that furnace, you have a free cremation.

Above the commander, behind the loader, and above the driver and radio-operator, there were escape hatches.

The commander, the driver and the radio-operator, worked the hydraulics.

As you unhooked them, they would pop open and swing to the side.

This enabled easy and quick access to get in or out of the panzer.

But…what you probably didn't know, was that they were not closed completely during battle.

They were locked with a pin, just before they were completely shut tight.

Why? Well, if you got a heavy grenade impact and you had to get out, the metal of the panzer could be deformed and then the hatch could be jammed, making it impossible to open and get out. You would become trapped and would probably die.

We managed to free Kovel from the Russians and liberate the German nurses, who were immediately put on transport back to Germany. Those girls were really exhilarated to get out of this precarious situation. They knew what would happen to them, if the Russians had captured them.

For us? Mission accomplished.

Because the city was not of any strategic value, because of the marshlands around it, we left it to the Russians again.

After Kovel, we had a relatively quiet period.

If panzers are not needed at the front, unlike infantry men who stay there most of the time, they were pulled back behind the frontlines.

Most of the time was for maintenance of machine and material.

We enjoyed the nice weather and, at the side of the road, we basked in the early summer sun of May.

Suddenly, our military reporter Bruno arrived and shouted: 'Mount up! We are moving!'

Within minutes each crew was up and ready to go.

In front of the line of panzers, stood the tank of the company commander.

He lifted his arm and made a circular movement.

The commanders behind him did so too, this was the signal to 'Start engines'

When all engines were running, the next move from the commander was to move his arm from high to low in a forward motion. That meant: 'Drive'

17 Panzers rumbled forward, what an incredible sight and sound to see and hear.

If you were outside a panzer, you would feel the earth trembling, long before you saw them coming. Awesome but incredible scary at the same time. A massive show of power which never failed to impress me, whether I was inside or outside the panzer.

In my time with the infantry, hearing a battalion of panzers approaching, I would try to find any hole I could find, to hide in.

It's that deep, loud roaring sound of the engine, the tracks rattling and the screeching sound of metal against metal, that gets to you and makes your legs feel like jelly.

Almost all infantry wants to get out of the way of an enemy tank. Myself included.

It turned out, we had to go back to the village of Kruhel.

Around 10 T-34's broke through our Wehrmacht defences and we had to destroy them.

It was clear territory and the T-34 is NO match for a Panzer on this terrain.

We could destroy them at a range of 2000 meters whilst the range of their guns was only 800 meters Without any losses we left 10 T-34's burning on the battlefield.

The next days we would have to battle with Russian tanks again, but this battle had made history; we even got mentioned in the journal of the 'Wehrmachtbericht' (Military Journal)

The Battle of Maciejowice or Maciejov as we so called it, started July 7th 1944.

Maciejowice is a small village about 70 kilometres to the South East of Warsaw.

My commander, Alfred Grossrock, would receive, for our outstanding performance in those days, the Knights Cross of Armour to the Iron Cross, the other 3 crewmembers received the Iron Class 2nd class and, because I already received Iron Class 2nd class, I automatically received Iron Cross 1st Class.

What happened that day? The Russians shot a humongous amount of fog grenades into our territory, they then launched an attack with a large amounts of tanks.

I think, it must have been 400 or 500 of them. Unbelievable to watch this happening in front of you.

We were "hull down", which meant our tank was behind a slope and only the turret was visible. Tacticaly and strategicaly, this was a very good defence position.

To our far left the tank of commander Ola Ulin, an NCO from Finland, began opening fire at the Russian tanks.

To our surprise something strange happened, the Russian tanks kept on moving towards the tank of Ola Ulin and, by doing so, the whole convoy of Russian tanks, oblivious of our presence, showed their flank to our position! So, of course, we opened fire on them.

It would be like a turkey shoot, wouldn't want to miss it.

Here was a golden opportunity to knock out a LOT of T-34's.

One Russian tank after the other, went up in flames or exploded , it was party time, at least for us it was. I don't think that day the Russians shared those feelings of exhilaration with us.

It looked like when we were happy, they were not.

Even though they sustained huge losses, the Russians kept on showing their flanks to us at a distance of only 500 meters.

We didn't know why? Why they didn't change direction? Why they didn't turn and come towards us? Face us, at least by doing so, they would probably have been able to cause some damage to us.

500 Meters distance was an ideal shooting range for us. Our gunner didn't even have to calculate the distance. Every shot was a hit and even worse it hit them in their flanks, their most vulnerable place. It was a complete tank massacre that day.

We guessed that after the battle , these were young and inexperienced soldiers.

Probably, they just assigned four people and put them in the T-34, which had just came off the assembly line. No experience, no practice and worst of all, probably no communication between their tanks on the battlefield.

They couldn't warn each other, they just kept going straight forwards. Driving straight to their doom.

In total, with help from the Wehrmacht, we destroyed 107 T-34's, of which our panzer alone destroyed 29 .

Our side, didn't even lose one tank. This outstanding performance was the reason our complete crew received their awards.

Well, the Russian may have had staggering losses, but it didn't seem to make much difference to their numbers. The very next day, so to speak, there would roll another 200 T-34's onto the battlefield.

We also noticed that they had been provided with American M4 Sherman tanks.

The American tanks were better equipped than the Russian ones. They all had radio communication and good seats, which the Russian T-34 lacked, when we had the chance to inspect one, on most occasions.

But, having said that, we would rather have fought against the Sherman's than the T-34, because the Sherman's armour was much weaker.

Somewhere in the month of July 1944, our panzer rolled slowly out of a forest, our commander gave the command; 'Halt'.

We stood on a slope and in front of us was clear territory, here and there a little house, but we could not detect any enemy movement.

The other panzers, behind us, also appeared on the edge of the forest and we formed our usual panzer formation, the W shape.

Three panzers in the front and two behind. This formation had proved the best way to attack and defend.

We were cautious. One whole army from the Wehrmacht had retreated or been captured by the Russians, we were directed to that empty area.

The situation with the German army was becoming rather catastrophic.

The panzer division of the Wehrmacht had just ONE panzer left, which had now been assigned to us.

We had 56 spare panzer crew members, but no panzers to assign them to.

Spare parts and therefore repairs to our panzers, had become rather a problem.

We advanced slowly and observed the area, wary of any kind of enemy action. Suddenly we came under an artillery attack.

It sounded like heavy 21 centimetre calibre. Those boys could inflict some serious damage!

The grenades exploded exactly in the area we were driving our panzers to. They exploded all around us. It was only a matter of time until some of us would receive a direct hit.

We couldn't figure out how that Russian artillery unit had pinpointed our position?

In front and at our back was a forest, so we were invisible until we came out into the open.

They must have an observer somewhere in the area to give them our coordinates?

Our commanders began looking through their binoculars, scanning the whole area around us.

Suddenly, commander Silvery shouted through the radio: 'I have spotted him, I have spotted him.'

Behind the forest in front of us, we saw the top of a tower.

The artillery observer held a position in the top of that tower.

Commander Silvery got the honours to take the guy out.

He'd better be quick, because the grenades were still dropping around us and were getting closer and closer.

Silvery turned his turret, lifted his canon, aimed and fired. With his 5th or 6th shot he made a spot on hit on the lookout position of the observer. Probably blew the guy to pieces.

Shortly after that the Russian artillery stopped firing.

Once more, the command was given to move on, we went in the direction of the forest in front of us.

We zigzagged through the forest, crushing the smaller trees and avoided the bigger ones.

We could have crushed the bigger ones too, but that would have taken more time.

At last, we arrived at a sizeable clearing, but the moment we entered this area, we came under fire from the Russian T-34's that had made a stand at the other side of the area.

By radio, I warned the other panzers behind us, so that they could prepare for this new situation.

Our commander told the driver; 'Pull up left and halt'.

By doing so we showed our front side at an angle towards the enemy.

In this position, you had a better chance that an incoming round would ricochet off the front sloping armour and would there for not penetrate the hull.

Our gunner got the next command; 'Enemy tank at 2 o'clock, distance 1200 meters'

The loader had already handed an anti-tank round to the gunner, switched the security of the round and the gunner reported; 'Target recognised' he fired immediately.

The T-34 was hit, just under the turret. The force of the explosion, lifted the turret up a bit and it landed, crooked, back on the tank.

Next command was for me 'Gunner, watch out for escapees.'

The only survivor of that tank, turned out to be the commander and he was mine.

With one burst of my MG34 he fell to the ground and didn't move.

Meanwhile, our other panzers merged with the battle and within a short time many of the Russian tanks were up in flames.

One or two T-34's made their escape, leaving 16 burned out T-34's on the battlefield.

We didn't lose a single panzer ourselves.

After this we had to make a halt, because Intel told us the forest in front of us, was full of Russian infantry and it would be suicidal to move our panzers into an area, without having backup from our infantry.

After a while, our supporting infantry unit arrived and climbed on the back of our panzers.

They loved to do this. First of all they didn't have to walk and secondly they felt safer and stronger, being ON the panzer.

This last part was absolutely not true, as I told you before in an earlier story.

With the infantry on the back of our panzers, we made a circular movement around the forest.

At the left side of the forest, there was a passage way, we could drive through.

As we moved into that open area, we sustained tremendous PAK fire.

The 623, which rode in front, immediately started to burn.

Our own infantry, leaving a couple of casualties behind, jumped off the panzers and ran back to the forest to find shelter.

Another one of our panzers got destroyed.

We started returning fire to the PAK stands, but after a third panzer lost its tracks, the commander ordered us to pull back. Too many PAK's in hiding. This was a game we couldn't win. Our infantry pulled back too.

Nobody wanted to be captured by the Russians. It would mean certain death.

I remembered that in the ice-cold winter of 1941-42, we re-conquered an area we had lost before to the Russians. We found German soldiers, naked, bound to the trees, covered with ice.

The Russians bound them to the trees, threw water over them and let them freeze to death.

With an outside temperature of -45, you wouldn't have a chance at all.

We saw more of those terrible atrocities, but I will not go into that any further.

After pulling back, we were re-directed to the Warsaw area.

The, so-called, wet triangle, where we had to make a stand.

12
AMBUSH

During the summer of 1944, the temperature outside my tank was scorching, But if it was hot outside the Panther, you can only imagine what the temperature was like inside. Even with the ventilator on full blast, it didn't really help lower the temperature. Only at night was it pleasantly cool. A panzer crew has to deal with two extremes. In the winter it was cold, only when driving did the engine heater provide you with some added warmth.. The moment you stopped and turned off the engine, this steel box became stone and stone cold. Well, let the engine running, I hear you say. Sadly, if not actually engaged in combat, we were prohibited from running the engine. We would wear as few clothes as possible. If we stopped, you could find a nice spot, somewhere in the shade, to take a rest. Considering the pro's and con's, I preferred the summer situation.

On July 20th we received a command to go to an area the Russian captured from us and that we had to take back again. It was a woody area, which we didn't like at all, because the enemy could hide himself everywhere without being noticed, until it was too late.

Our panzer had the 'honour' today to drive at the head of the convoy. This always made me a bit nervous,

because you are always the first target the enemy gets into his sights.

As we followed down a dirt road, meanwhile we would constantly look around us for signs of danger.

The road got narrower as we travelled down on it And, about 3 kilometres in front of us, we noticed a little village. Suddenly, a big bang sounded throughout our panzer. The sound can be compared to sitting in an oil barrel while somebody hits it with a baseball bat. Deafening, really. At first we thought we were hit by enemy fire and we expected another impact quickly after the first one. But it didn't come. Our commander informed us about our situation. We had run over an anti-tank mine and couldn't drive any further. By radio, I informed the panzers behind us to take note and be careful. The Germans always laid their mines in a special pattern, but the Russians just laid them at random without any system at all.

Even though I warned the panzers behind us, two of them also hit mines, after they had passed by our panzer.

I contacted the mechanic group, who were always following the convoy. The mechanics reported to us that they could fix the other two panzers, but ours was irreparable due to the fact that our left drive wheel was totally destroyed and they would have to tow the panzer to the workshop to be able to fix that. The other two panzers only had broken tracks that could be replaced 'easily'. To do that you had to loosen the track tensioner. After the tracks were loosened, they had to hammer out the bolts of the broken track parts, to separate it from the rest of the tracks. All Panthers had spare tracks on their sides. First, a new piece was put into the area that had to be replaced and the bolts were hammered back again to connect the new track on one side to the old track. Next, with a tow cable, the repaired track would be put back into place and, by turning the front drive wheel, it was pulled further forwards. Now the two ends of the tracks had to be connected together by hammering back the last bolts. All in all, this was a very hard laborious job. If this was done, the track tensioner pulled the track into the right tension and the job was done. Ready to rock and roll again. All in all this job took several hours and the remaining panzers of our group were already engaged in battle with some Russian PAK's, which were hidden a little bit further down the road. They managed to destroy 5 PAK stands and a couple of T-34s, who also tried desperately to join this party. We even took some Russian prisoners, who were stitting on the ground in their typical brown-green uniforms.

A tow panzer towed our panzer away, and we were promised we would get it back the very next day. Without the protection of our Panther we felt 'naked'. The only weapons we had were our pistols and those would not help much if the enemy chose to attack again. Then, our loader started to complain about a severe headache. It turned out that the heavy explostion had made him hit his head against the turret wall. Later, he was diagnosed with a concussion.

Next day, we went to the workshop, together with a replacement loader, to pick up our repaired Panther. Immediately after that they directed us to Czeremcha, a village close to the (now) Polish-Russian border about 190 kilometers to the east from Warsaw. The Russians had captured this territory and we had to get them out of there. Around that time I was a crewmember, together with Alfred Grossrock our commander, of Panther 611. Two weeks later, after our own company commander, Martin, died, Grossrock became the new company commander and we all were transferred to Panther 600, the company commander panzer. All panzers, ending on two zeros, were company commander panzers. This is just a little technical side information, but now back to the real deal: the battle.

We attacked the village Czeremcha in the flank, which was a direction the Russians didn't expect us to come from, so we gained territory very quickly and managed to to take Czeremcha from the Russians.

Because our 1st division panzers also took part of the battle, we had a total of 100 panzers. With the help of regiments Westland and Germania we managed to occupy the whole zone around Czeremcha. Two of our panzers were out of combat again, due to mines, and three panzers from 1st battalion suffered the same fate. We were always surprised how quickly the Russians managed to mine a whole area before they retreated. Many more things about the Russians surprised us,like the wooden bridge over the Narew river. The amazing thing about this bridge was that it was built just under the surface of the water. Even our airplanes couldn't detect it and the Russians were able to transport men and material at night from one side to the other.

After the battle of Czeremcha, a couple of calm weeks lay ahead of us. Around August 1th 1944 we were quartered around the city of Stanyslaviv. If you want to look it up: after 1962 they renamed it into Ivano-Frankivsk. Our convoy was patrolling the area with the assignment to spot and destroy Russian troops that had broken through our lines. We drove, cautious and watchful, through a forest and at the end of the forest we saw a little house to our right. At that moment a loud bang and, again, we lost, this time, the right front drive wheel due to a grenade hit. A fire fight followed immediately after that. Four tanks, showing their flanks to our side, appeared out in the open and three of them were destroyed immediately, One of them turned out to be an American Sherman tank, but the fourth tank choose wisely to retreat quickly.

Now we had, again, an immobilised panzer and we had to wait, again, on a tow back panzer to bring the Panther to the workshop. Alfred Grossrock, decided not to wait. He took command over another panzer and drove away to complete his assignment.

Together with the mechanics, who always drove behind the panzers, we managed to shortcut the track, so the panzer would be ready for tow back. After this job was done, we had to follow our panzer convoy, with the 'Muli' ('Maultier' Half-track Truck).This was a truck with wheels in the front and tracks in the back. The driver of the mechanics truck was a Dutch guy, named Chris Vliegen. Three men would stay behind to guard our immobilized Panther. I decided to take my place on the footboards of the truck, next to the driver, as we drove away. The backside of the truck was covered with canvas and that made a stay over there, with the heat of the day, not comfortable at all. Besides, now I could talk Dutch again, standing next to Chris, the driver. Meanwhile, I put my pistol in the driver's cabin of the truck.

We passed a very small village and after this, the road made a curve and, in that curve, we saw a still burning halftrack German S.P.W or so called Schutzenpanzerwagen, or 'Armoured Troop Carrier', from our Germania division. One Panzer grenadier battalion in each Panzer division was equipped with these to allow them to accompany the panzers. We drove around it and went on our way, but in hindsight, we should have known better, because this turned out to be an terribly incorrect decision.

I was just having a casual conversation with Chris, the driver, as we heard machinegun shots. My first thought was an airplane attack? I jumped from the foot board to take cover at the other side of the car, as the door on that side opened and immediately three men tumbled out, Chris being the fourth and last. When he passed me by, he shouted: 'Russians!' after which he Immediately disappeared. It started to be dusk already and it was difficult to get a clear picture what the hell was going on here? Then, I noticed, looking around me, a house and at the right side of it, foxholes with Russian infantry in them. This all happened in a split second and my mind gave me only one order: RUN!

To the men in the back of our truck, I shouted: "Russians" and I hurried away, finding myself running through a potato field. Very quickly, fear gives you wings, and I managed to outrun the other four guys from the front cabin of the truck. It turned out to be Vliegen, the driver, Landwehr, the head of the mechanics, Schirrmeister, in charge of car fleet, and Richer, a guy I never met before.

Schirrmeister had never "sniffed the air" from the battlefield and claimed he was "dying" to have this experience.

Well, he got what he wished for and by doing so, also sustained a small injury in his leg from some shrapnel. Bleeding only slightly, I guessed he wanted to be awarded the Knights Cross!

At this moment we still were in danger of getting hit by stray bullets, because the Russians were shooting like crazy and it didn't look like they would stop any time soon. So, we kept on running, until we were well out of the danger zone. Shortly after that, we heard somebody behind us, gasping for breath. It turned out to be Walter Heger, one of the guys out of the back of the truck. He told us what happened to them, after we made our hasty escape to save our lives.

After hearing me yelling: 'Russians' panic broke out amidst the six or seven men in the back of our truck and everyone wanted to get out as soon as possible. First one to get out was a young guy, named Werner. He encountered a Russian, standing already at the back of the truck, who shot him through his stomach. Werner tumbled, badly wounded, out of the truck, onto the ground. After him came Walter, who pointed his, still secured, rifle to the Russian, who ducked away, not knowing the rifle wasn't ready to shoot. By ducking away, Walter grabbed the opportunity to jump out of the truck and get the hell out of there. Behind him, he heard the sound of exploding hand grenades. Probably the Russians didn't want to take any risks and threw a couple of hand grenades in the back of the truck. Until now these men were reported as MIA, Missing In Action.

We decided to walk back to the spot where we left our panzer. Of the five men who jumped out of the truck, Chris and I were the only two with battle experience. By now it was pitch dark and very difficult to find your way. Finally, we reached the spot where we left our panzer. All was quiet. Strange? It gave us that eerie feeling something must be wrong? To our surprise, the three men we left behind, were all sleeping behind the panzer! No guards, nothing? Nerves of steel or just plain stupid? If you ask me: plain stupid! We awoke them and told them what happened. After assigning some of them to guard duty, the rest of us went to sleep.

We all felt distinctly uneasy because now there was no line of defence between us and the Russians. In the middle of the night, the guard awoke me, whispering nervously, that he heard somebody coming. I closed my eyes, listened and indeed, he was right, something or somebody was coming our way.

I heard the sounds of heavy footsteps in the sand and with my heart bouncing in my throat, I shouted: 'Halt, Make yourself known.' The sound stopped abruptly and I grabbed his rifle out of the guard's hands and began walking in the direction where the sound was coming from. Suddenly, in front of me, there was a horse. It gave me almost a heart attack! Probably it escaped somewhere and now was just wandering around. I sighed with relief and went back to sleep. Next morning, at the crack of dawn, we went on our way to catch up with the rest of our division. While busy doing that, we encountered a battalion of panzers from the Totenkopf Division, who had orders to follow Wiking division. With all that steel between us and the Russians, we felt more secure. At the end of the day, we managed to get back to our division and, of course, had to report all that had happened.

Our division managed to destroy or capture all the Russians, who had broken through our lines. And also, our repaired Panther came back. The maintenance crew had changed the front drive wheel in just one day. It was good to sit in my familiar seat again. But meanwhile, the Russians gained strength by endless new supplies of men and materials. In addition, they also had new planes in abundance, many of them from the USA. Unfortunately, our side could hardly expect air support anymore. Once in a while, you saw a lonely Messerschmitt 109 or 110, roaming through the sky. That was it. Half of our armies were now in Normandy and Italy to push back the Allies over there. The strength of Wiking division dwindled back down from 9000 men, to a meager 2200 men. Also, the number of our panzers was in rapid decline.

The pressure became so great that the only thing we could do was retreat, retreat and retreat again. But we knew that this state of affairs couldn't go on like this indefinitely.Near the city of Siemiatycze, we crossed the river Bug and entered the Wet Triangle, so called because this is where the rivers Bug, Narew and Weichsel flow together, where we had to make a definite stand.

13
SILVERY

We were situated somewhere in the Warsaw area. It was a nice warm day and our division of panzers made quarter in a forest.

Normally tanks don't like to be there, but with more and more enemy fighter planes above us, we stayed under cover, only to come out when needed.

In front of this forest, our infantry made their quarters. It was quiet everywhere. Too quiet, if you would ask me. It looked like that silence before a big storm would hit you.

And of course, suddenly, Russian artillery started blasting their guns.

Too our luck, their impacts were far in front of us, so nobody panicked or took shelter at this time.

Some even stayed basking in the sun.

As a veteran you know what calibre of gun they are firing, you hear the sound of the incoming grenades and you know: those are blowing over or they are too short, too far right or too far left.

But this time, the shooting increased and also our own artillery decided to be a part of this loud game.

Sadly, our artillery shells were rationed. This may sound odd in wartime, but many of the factories in Germany, that manufactured our shells, had been bombed and were either partially or completely destroyed.

We also were rationed in the use of gasoline/petrol for our panzers.

The German panzers ran on gasoline, the Russian tank engines used diesel fuel.

Our Panther consumed a staggering 800 litres (212 gallons) to drive only 100 kilometres in the field.

Talking about the Russian artillery: In my opinion this unit was the best trained of the whole Russian army. They were good, very good and accurate.

Their tank crews and infantry units, by the way, were just worthless.

The only way they made their presence countable was because of their huge numbers.

Well, I guess, that's how you win a conventional war, isn't it?

Just throw in enough material, men and absolutely don't care how much material and men that you lose. That's how the Russians did it and eventually, it paid off.

The fact that our artillery started shooting, meant that we would get the signal 'Action' pretty soon.

That thought hadn't even left my mind or the order was already shouted 'Aufsitzen', which literally means 'mount', like you would get on a horse.

It doesn't sound so strange, if you consider tanks were part of the cavalry units.

Although horses were, more or less, becoming obsolete, nevertheless, the army component, that formerly fought with horses, and later with tanks, was still called 'cavalry',

After all our panzer engines were roaring, it always gave me goose bumps and chills, running through my spine.

It was such a massive display of power, and it never failed to impress me.

But, at the other side, I also always felt nervous for our next assignment; support our infantry units and destroy the Russian tanks.

As we advanced, the nervousness feeling slowly went away and by the time we went into combat, it would be completely gone.

I already knew myself pretty well, after years of experience and being in combat, it would always go like this.

The Russian artillery followed us exactly wherever we went.

This was logical, because our panzers were the greatest threat for them.

The moment we reached the H.K.L (Haupt Kampf Linie) or Main Line of Fighting, we immediately draw fire from some Russian tanks that were cruising through our infantry units.

The first tank we aimed on, was straight in front of us, showing his flank.

Distance was just a mere 100 metres.

Our gunner hit him directly in the flank.

A massive explosion followed, as the tank exploded, there were no survivors in that crew.

Now other Russian tanks also started burning, due to the action of our other panzers.

Here and there, some crewmembers managed to crawl out of their burning and destroyed tanks, but that didn't mean they were safe.

The infantry and us, the machine gunners from the panzers, shot at everybody that made it out alive of those Russian tanks. That may sound cruel, but believe me, the other way around it would be the same ballgame. No surrender and no mercy granted over here.

After this fight our company commander, Martin, took some Russian prisoners and wanted to transport them, in his convertible vehicle, behind the front lines for further interrogation.

There would be a translator available, to hear from them about future plans of their army units.

They never reached their destination though.

One of those Russians POW, carried a hidden hand grenade with him and blew himself, his three comrades and everybody else in the car, except the driver, to kingdom come.

That must have been one fanatical S.O.A.B (excuse my language).

The loss of commander Martin was, for us, tragic, because he was, besides being a good leader, a much loved and respected person. After this tragic accident, my commander Alfred Grossrock, took over as company commander and therefore our whole crew transferred from Panther 611, to the company commander Panther 600. (double zero at the end; means the panzer of a company commander).

In the meantime, time went on and as we write it was August 18th 1944.

Higher command had let us retreat a little, to straighten out the frontlines.

The Russians were pretty quiet, but we knew that wouldn't last, it never did.

They were gathering strength to make a move, we suspected to go northwest, and then, in one go, they would move straight forward, until they would reach the East sea and, by doing this, complete an encirclement movement around our whole army.

We only could wait and see what would happen. The Initiative, around this time of the war, most of the time, was not on our side any longer.

Suddenly, heavy artillery firing started.

This time, it really looked like the whole world was exploding.

As usual, artillery fire starts shooting at our infantry, in front of us, and gradually would move backwards, therefore making us their next target.

But, we still had time before it would hit us. At least, we thought we had.

Our crew was still busy in doing all the recreational things they normally did.

Nobody was in a hurry to take cover in their panzers, yet.

Commander Silvery, the one that took out the tower with the Russian observer in it, had an urgent call from nature, and under the slogan 'If you got to go, you got to go' he hurried to the forest to relieve himself.

Suddenly, and earlier as expected, the artillery fire came towards us. Everybody started to run and got in their panzers as quickly as possible.

On moments like these, there was nothing more we could do, only wait and sit this one out.

Suddenly, over the radio, the order came to move forward and assist our infantry units.

Our infantry troops sighed with relief, when they saw their panzers arriving at the battlefield to give them support.

They felt a lot safer, with that wall of steel between them and the Russians.

Without any loses of our own, we managed to destroy 14 T-34's and while we're busy doing that, we also ruined the life of many Russian infantry men. It was all in a day's work.

After their heavy losses the remaining Russian tanks tried to leave the battlefield, but three more of them were taken out by our carefully hidden PAK units.

The famous German tank commander Michael Wittman always said: 'A destroyed enemy tank counts for one kill, but a destroyed enemy PAK counts for TWO!' and I think he was right about that. We feared enemy PAK units far more then enemy tanks, due to their stealthy operation.

Well, the battle came to an end.

The Russian infantry retreated with the remainders, of what was left, of their tanks. Finally our infantry units could breathe in relief.

Of course we had dead men and wounded to worry about, but that was 'normal'.

Statistics told us, for every dead soldier, there would be four more of them wounded.

At the end, in history, a whole war is brought down to only statistics and numbers.

We went back to our old quarter, only to find out that commander Silvery's Panther was still standing there? During the whole battle it hadn't moved from his spot? Seeing and hearing us, the crew came out of their Panther and informed us what happened.

They told us, that after the artillery shooting, they looked for him everywhere, but he was nowhere to be found?

We helped them searching again and walked through the forest, where Silvery last was sighted.

We noticed the Russian artillery fire had done a lot of damage to the forest.

Many trees were broken or totally destroyed and it was our guess that commander Silvery, busy in relieving himself, got a direct hit by a shell and was blown to smithereens.

There was nothing left of him anywhere to be found. No traces at all.

If you got to go, you got to go and he went. I guess, in hindsight, it's not even a bad way to go either. One moment you're there, and the next you are completely gone. No pain, no suffering at all. Just..... gone.

Around night time, we already got a replacement for Silvery and life went on like nothing really happened.

It's peculiar, now, now I'm old, I often think back to all those comrades, who died so young and in a violent way.

At that time, I hardly grieved about them, or better said, I didn't allow myself to grieve about them. Mentally it would get the best of you, if you would grieve about every lost comrade (too many).

You had to 'switch off' your emotions in order to go on. It was so 'normal' to be confronted with dead and loss every day.

Somebody died and they expected you to go back to business as usual. But not every person was able to 'switch himself off' and some of our soldiers, who weren't able to 'switch off', couldn't cope with all this tragedy on a daily basis and they got a mental problems.

In that time, PTSD, or Post Traumatic Stress Disorder, was never heard off.

It first became the diagnosis, as we know it today, in 1980.

In the second WW, I think, they called it 'Shell Shock'.

Note: In 1941 Abram Kardiner, an American psychanalyst, states, that battle neurosis, battle fatigue, combat exhaustion and shell shock are all and the same.

Later, after I wrote, on request of my son, my diaries about this period, he asked me why the stories I wrote, lacked any emotion?

I told him, I couldn't write any of it down, if I would let my emotions get involved. It would only paralyze my memories and writing capacities, so in order to recall all those memories I still had to keep myself 'switched off'.

Note: In fact my father stayed his whole life 'switched off' and, by doing so, he was able to work, lead a normal life, be a normal husband and father and never showed any signs of PTSD. Only at night, in his dreams, once in a while, when he couldn't control the 'switch' he would get nightmares, screaming 'They attack us, they attack us from the left side'. My mother would awake him, calm him down and he went back to sleep again. Back to business as usual.

If a panzer unit had to be transported over a longer distance, it would be done by train, just to save fuel and engines.

We were unloaded at a station in the area of Brest-Litovsk (now known as Brest) which is close to the Polish border.

Only now, did they tell us why we were here.

Our whole second army had been destroyed by a huge Russian military force.

The German soldiers were either, killed, captured or had ran away and now there was a gap of 100 kilometres length in the front lines.

We could never ever close this gap, being only one division, so more divisions would follow us, but, like most of the times, we always were the first to enter the party. We called ourselves jokingly 'The Fire Brigade', because our division was always directed first to a battle scene.

The weather, by the way, was beautiful, but hot.

If you would touch the outside of our Panther, you would burn your hands and you could actually fry an egg on it.

Within the Panther, it was like an oven. If not moving, you wouldn't want to be inside.

The area where we made quarter, was a wooded area and as long there was no war going on, it was really beautiful and peaceful.

You could hear the birds in the trees and many of us were sleeping in the shades of those trees. Suddenly, we received the familiar command 'Aufsitzen' (mount) and we all hurried to our spots in the panzers.

I switched on my transmitter and receiver (10 Watt transmitter Caesar and U.K.W, ultra-short wave band, receiver Emil).

Our line of panzers swung around a bend in the road, it was such a long line of panzers you actually couldn't see the first panzer in line.

On the roads and through the little villages we passed, it was all quiet, nobody to see or hear.

In war time this is eerie and means, most of the time, that trouble is lying ahead.

After driving half an hour, we arrived at a deserted village, in which we made a stop.

There was some infantry from the Wehrmacht (regular army) and a 7.5 cm PAK, that would be able to throw a decent punch to any T-34 that would try to come near.

Later, we called this village, the carrot village, because all the fields surrounding it, were full with carrots. We went into the fields, picked and cooked them and they tasted delicious.

This village would be our stand and meanwhile another PAK arrived from the Wehrmacht to join the first one.

A little later, we saw in a distance, a group from our 'Aufklarungs-abteilung' (A.A) translates as 'Reconnaissance Battalion' coming towards our position.

If those guys from our Wehrmacht didn't recognise their own army, or they were just a bunch of idiots? I will never know, but they started shooting at them.

Those guys from the A.A. didn't understand what was happening and started, on their turn, to shoot an explosive shell towards us.

This shell turned out to be a deadly hit for our mechanic, Richard Binar.

He was one of the guys from the maintenance truck, that always followed the panzer units to support them with any mechanical failure or problems.

I wired a message to the A.A. unit, that this was a case of so called 'friendly fire' and also the PAK unit was informed, but it was all but too late for Richard Binar.

Binar and myself never could get along very well and I never knew a reason for that.

After the war, I heard from the other surviving guys, who also knew him, he couldn't get along with anybody at all. He was a grumbler and crossed paths with almost anyone, but…hey…he didn't have to die for that?

The A.A. unit informed us there were no Russians in the area in front of us.

We moved on and passed several small villages, until we made a stop for quarter.

We had to manoeuvre our Panther to a sheltered place and camouflage it with branches, so it wouldn't be noticed by enemy planes.

Because dusk was setting in and visibility became poor for our driver, I climbed out our panzer to guide him, by giving directions where to manoeuvre.

Walking backwards, I made arm movements, like a little forwards, a little bit to the left, now a little bit to the right, but, I didn't notice that on the floor, there was a wooden pole from a nearby broken fence.

The tracks of the panzer rolled over the pole, lifted it up and, when it shot out from under the tracks, it landed exactly on my head, knocking me out, just in front of the tracks of our, still forwards moving, panzer. Our driver, because of bad visibility in the panzer, didn't see any of this happen.

He didn't see me anymore, so he thought, I must have stepped aside.

I would have been crushed completely, if it wasn't for our loader.

He saw the whole thing happening and warned our driver to stop the panzer, just inches before it would have run over me.

Even now, so many years later, I still get goose bumps, thinking I could have lost my life just by this stupid accident.

But that was just what happened most of the time. You go to the woods, to take a crap and you get blown to smithereens by a shell. Most of those things were just coincidences, combined with bad luck.

Sadly our loader, Paul Kustner, the one who just saved my life, lost his own life on March 22nd 1945, when the Russians destroyed our Panther.

The next day, we had to move further and during our advance nothing happened. It looked we were on a holiday trip?

The loader, gunner and me used this opportunity to get out of the tank, as it still drove, and we made a comfortable quarter on the backside of our panzer.

You could enjoy a nice cool breeze over there and, lying on our backs, we could spot for enemy planes approaching.

There was no sign at all from our former H.K.L and it looked like the war had ended? But it hadn't.

One day we made quarter in an empty village, again.

Dusk was setting in, as we saw a big dust cloud coming towards our position.

It turned out to be a convoy of trucks. Germans? Russians? We couldn't tell yet.

We watched the convoy come closer and then we saw it: Russians!

Probably they were lost or they thought, just like us, this was not occupied territory.

Big mistake!

Now everybody reacted with lightning speed.

We aimed at the first truck, to stop the convoy. The shell hit the engine of the truck and staggering it came to a stop.

Now we targeted the last truck, so it would block the exit road for the others. That truck was set ablaze.

The other trucks bumped into each other and the chaos was complete.

Now the remaining drivers tried to turn their trucks to get the hell out of there, but they were unable to.

From the top of our panzers we started to empty our machineguns at them.

The survivors tried to flee into the fields, but we didn't allow them to do that.

Our machineguns kept firing, until we couldn't detect a single movement over there.

Coming closer, we saw and heard around 20 survivors, moaning in the fields.

After we took care of the wounded, they were transported to the back with a couple of infantry as guards.

Now it was time to check out the trucks. They all turned out to be American Dodge's.

But also the freight they carried, turned out to be American and even better, K-rations!

Fully loaded with biscuits, chocolate, cigarettes etcetera.

We never were able to lay our hands on so many supplies before and every nook and cranny of our panzers and uniforms were filled with what we took from those trucks.

The rest we sent, together with the still working trucks, back to our supply unit, so others would also benefit from this present.

In the meanwhile we received the message that the Russian army had indeed almost moved around the south of Warsaw and we had to get the hell out of here, or we would be encircled, like the Cherkassy pocket all over again.

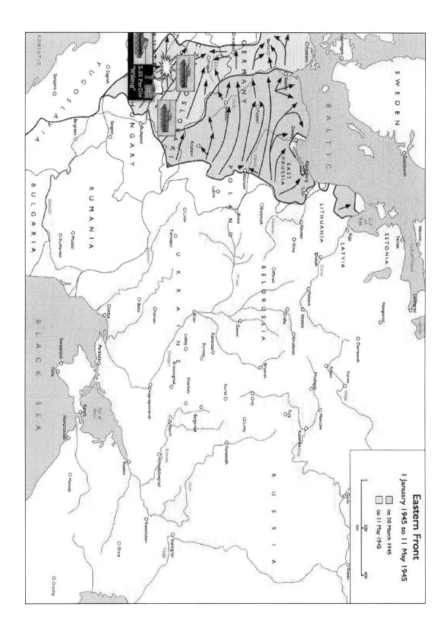

14

HANS HEUFFLER

tanyslaviv (now known as Ivano-Frankivsk) lay straight ahead of us and only a large forest separated us from the city. The Russians had taken it from us and we had to take it back again because of its strategic roads. The High Command gave us a battalion of infantry from the Westland regiment and High Command assumed that together, we could do the job.

The infantry climbed upon our panzers and we drove over an open spot through the forest, nearing a more densely grown area on the other side without any warning, we started to receive incoming fire. The Russians had already pulled up until the edge of the forest. Our infantry immediately jumped off the panzers and looked for cover.

One or more of the infantry men were probably wounded because over the radio I heard somebody call for a medic. Next, out of nowhere, ten Russian fighter planes arrived on the scene and started shooting at us and dropped their bombs. Luckily for us, they all fell and exploded in the forest to the left of us. Only our infantry sustained casualties and had some wounded men after the air attack.

When the planes left, our infantry regrouped and started their attack on the Russian lines.

Our infantry spread out in a wide line and at random, a couple of them jumped up, ran a couple of meters and dropped down again. This was followed by another couple soldiers, jumping up and advancing a couple of meters before dropping down again. By doing this, you minimize the risk of being wiped out by enemy machine gun fire.

Before they could aim at us, the target was already gone and suddenly, somewhere else, infantry men popped up. Using our machine guns, we fired over the heads of our infantry men to give them cover. We gave short bursts of fire and you had to be very careful not to hit your own men.

The panzer gunners shot some explosive rounds at the Russians, just to make the party complete. Due to the rounds exploding against the trees, a hail of wood and steel splinters came down on those enemy soldiers.

My commander ordered me, to contact our artillery unit, to launch a strike on the Russians in front of us. As long as they still had infantry men over there, it was not advisable for our panzers to move in. The Russians could easily take us out with, sticky mines, Panzerfausts (German Bazooka) or Molotov cocktails. The Russians, if they managed to get hold of them, used our own Panzerfausts against us, which seemed to me to be bitter in getting killed by a weapon manufactured by your own military. After the artillery got their coordinates, they released a barrage of explosive bombs on the Russian lines and again a hail of metal and wood came down on those Russians in the forest, but much worse than we had ever inflicted on them before. We could also hear the screaming of the wounded Russians.

Our artillery moved their fire from the left to the right and back again, so nobody, on the side of the Russians, could complain afterwards that they had been forgotten. We tried to treat them all equally. Even a foxhole couldn't protect you from this barrage of explosions, they were open at the top and all the danger came from above.

One after another, accompanied by our infantry, our panzers start to move into the forest. In the forest, we encountered many dead and wounded Russians. The wounded men all sustained injuries from the wooden and steel debris flying around. The Russians decided to retreat and therefore we could advance through the forest, knocking down trees all around us.

The moment we entered a clearing, we received an insane amount of shooting from Russian PAK (anti- tank cannons). Our panzer sustained a number of 'hits' and became immobile.

Our commander threw out a 'fog grenade' and gave the order: 'Ausbooten' which means 'Leave the Panzer'. The good part of the shooting from the Russian PAK units was, that we now knew their positions.

The other panzers from our group used this opportunity and launched explosive rounds to destroy all nine of their PAKs. Our infantry men, who had been hugging the earth during this shooting, got up and regrouped with the rest of their unit.

However at this moment, on the other side of the clearing, five Sherman tanks appeared out of the forest. Clearly, they had no clue as to our presence and calmly crossed the open field from the left to the right! Well, a better target you could hardly wish for and this looked like an early Christmas present to us. The distance was a mere 1000 metres and our commander quickly gave the order to the rest of our panzers to engage the enemy. By this time, only a handful of our panzers emerged out of the forest but it was enough to do the job. One of our panzers aimed at the Sherman tank on the far left and another one of our panzers aimed at the one on the far right.

Shots rang and before we could determine the effect of it, we reloaded and aimed at the other Sherman's.

The Sherman we hit first, exploded with a mighty 'Bang'. Its turret went up sky-high and landed a few meters from the tank. Needless to say, the Sherman's were no match at all for the Panthers .

When we next moved towards the carnage in front of us, we noticed some crew members had survived and were desperately trying to crawl out of their destroyed tanks.

We fired our machineguns at them but because we were still on the move, this had no effect at all. By the time our infantry arrived at the scene of the crime, the surviving crew members had already disappeared into the forest behind them. However there were some wounded Russian crew members left at their tanks. One of them lay down, next to his destroyed tank and as we approached him, he quickly pulled out a gun and shot one of our crew members through his shoulder.

We never appreciated jokes like this, so it was also the last action he ever undertook.

We shot him on the spot. Why he would do this? It was probably because he was afraid.

Being wounded, he probably feared, he would be executed anyhow and acted out in a last desperate attempt. The rest of the wounded men, all with burn wounds, which is very common for tank crew members, became POWs and were brought back behind our lines.

After our mechanics had repaired our Panther, we were back in the game again.

The forest in front of us, had the shape of a long finger, and we noticed there was a gap on the left side of it, were the Sherman's had entered their last field of play, this would enable us to circle around the forest and therefore be more in the open. Tanks like to be out in the open.

As the convoy of our panzers, slowly and carefully, moved alongside this 'long finger' forest, we looked carefully around us, so as to detect any enemy movement.

All went well, until we reached the top of 'the long finger' and wanted to go around it. In front of us appeared a clear open field and another forest behind that. At the exact moment we went round the corner, we received heavy PAK firing again. Due to our position as first in line, we were the first to get hit.

After more panzers appeared on the battlefield, the Russian PAKs had to divide, luckily for us, their attention. Now everybody got their fair share. As I told you before; we all liked to be treated equally.

Even though our ventilators were working at full speed, the combination of powder fumes and the heat, let us gasp for air inside our panzer.

On top of this, on the Russian side, a couple of T-34s decided, they too wanted to be a part of this battle. Pretty soon a fierce fight between enemy tanks and PAK units followed.

Our other panzers passed our panzers and they concentrated on taking out the T-34s as we concentrated on taking out the PAKs.

Our panzers had the advantage, because we were directly opposite the enemy tanks and the Panther could take a lot more hits on his front armour, compared to the T-34.

At this distance they couldn't even penetrate our armour at all and we could still destroy them.

Only our tracks and front drive wheels could be destroyed by them.

Meanwhile another ten T-34s arrived on the scene, we now had so many targets to choose from!

By now, the banging of all those guns and rounds was deafening. One after another, the T-34s went up in flames. The surviving crew members tried to save their lives, but our infantry shot at everybody who managed to get out of a Russian tank. Now the Russians tried to retreat, but by doing so, they showed their flanks to us. This is always a bad decision and pretty soon they turned into a crematorium of burning fuel and ammunition.

If WE had to retreat, we didn't just turn around and show our vulnerable flank or backsides.

No, we used fog grenades for cover, used the backward gears to get out of the line of fire and THEN we turned around and therefore managed to avoid being destroyed.

Again, it showed a lack of training of those Russian tank crews.

The Russian Pak was already destroyed and only Russian infantry were left.

Suddenly, we saw a Russian, with a very long rifle jump out of the forest and make a run to one of the ditches in front of him. This particular rifle had a very large calibre bullet. The Russians used it as an anti-tank weapon. Against our lighter armoured panzers and vehicles, this weapon could make the difference, but to use it against a Panther or a Tiger? Come on. No way. Or you really had to get very close to our Panther.

That Russian guy must have been completely crazy or a hell of a patriot, to try this all by himself.

We waited for him but It took a while before he popped up again out of the ditch. Stupidly, he did this at the same spot as where he jumped into the ditch. This was a big tactical mistake. Our PAK aimed an explosive round at that spot where this guy jumped into the ditch. Had he moved a little to the left or the right, he would have surprised us. Now, only a big bang sounded from our PAK and the Russian was lifted up into the air, together with his toy gun, and dropped, like a sack of potatoes, dead to the ground.

At the end of August 1944, we were, closed in by the Russians, after an attack. This is never a comfortable position to find yourself in, I can tell you. They advanced with a large amount of troops and, by doing this, encircled us. Meanwhile, it was night and we had no infantry support, so we had to be very careful not to be surprised by the Russian infantry. They could use sticky mines or some other anti-tank devices and ruin our day. Also our artillery were still rationed. They were not allowed to fire freely anymore. They could only do this in cases of emergency.

Well, in my opinion, the whole German frontline was one big case of an emergency around this time, but nobody took advice from us.

Our commander gave the order to try and escape this encirclement. In front of us, we saw an overpass and as intel told us, going under that overpass, would bring us into friendly territory and therefore into safety. So, our group of panzers moved in that direction. Our panzer was the first in line. This is always the less desirable position, but everybody got their turn at that position.

Just after we went through the overpass, I saw two bright lights and after that I heard a loud 'Bang' and our panzer came to a complete stop. Something had hit us! Probably a captured German Panzerfaust, now used by the Russians against us. Oh, what irony! We had to get out of our Panther as soon as possible. An immobile panzer, in enemy territory, is a sitting duck, waiting to be killed.

The crew in the turret could escape easily, by means of the hatch at the back of the loader but for us, the driver and me, it was more dangerous. Our hatch was on the top deck, in the front of the panzer. If we would open it, we would be in plain sight of the enemy. Meanwhile it had turned dark already. That would be to our benefit. Instead of releasing the pin of the hatch, the driver and I decided to hold the hatch, so it would not swing open and make a lot of noise. The last thing we wanted, was to draw any attention from the Russians opposite us.

We opened our hatches by hand and slowly, let them pop up and very carefully guided them to the side. We managed to do this without making any sounds. We then pulled ourselves up out of our positions. We expected enemy fire at any moment, but nothing happened. Next, we crawled over the turret and once on the other side, we jumped to the ground. The other three crew members were already waiting for us.

For the time being, we were pretty safe because our panzer blocked the way through the overpass. The Russians could only get to us, if they were stupid enough to climb over the panzer. They didn't.

While we were just walking back to our other panzers, a loud explosion and a blaze of fire marked the end of our Panther. The Russians finished their job and we had escaped just in time.

We found shelter with our other panzers and it was only at dawn, when we managed to escape through the encirclement, due to the help from an outside German panzer group, who managed to break through the encirclement and set us free.

Once back with our unit, we got a new Panther (very rare already) and that made us happy.

Nowadays, material was very scarce and many panzer crews were left without a panzer and were reassigned to the infantry units. We didn't want that to happen, so we were glad to get a new Panther.

At one point, we even started to use captured T-34s, marked them as German, and went into battle with them. Meanwhile, the Russians didn't give up trying to circle around Warsaw and get to the East Sea. We constantly tried to prevent this from happening.

These fights, that lasted until December 1944, came to be known as the battle of the Wet Triangle because in that area three rivers merged together.

We managed to, even with our greatly diluted 6th company, on 30th August 1944, destroy another twenty T-34s but they kept on coming and coming.

On the second day of Christmas 1944, they awoke us and announced that we would be moved by train. They transported the whole panzer battalion, by use of special panzer trains, but we had no clue where they were sending us? They never told us. Information was always on 'a need to know' basis, and I think, most of the time higher command thought, there was no need?

We knew the Russians were getting ready for a major attack, so why they moved us out of that area, we couldn't figure out.

When the train entered Germany, it puzzled us even more.

Are we going to Italy? As we were moving to the south and we knew in Italy there was heavy fighting going on. It didn't seem logical to us, because Wiking mainly consisted of volunteers who only wanted to fight on the East Front. After entering the Czech republic, we guessed our destination: Budapest, the capital of Hungary. This was due to the encirclement of the city by the Russians. A delicate situation was at hand.

Hans Heuffler, one of the few good friends I had left and panzer commander of the 635, sat next to me and told me he would be given a leave of absence pretty soon and asked me, if he could borrow my panzer uniform. The one he had, was in a terrible state and he wanted to make an immaculate impression to his friends and family in his hometown, somewhere in Tirol of Austria. He knew, I had two uniforms. I claimed my former uniform as burned, when our panzer was destroyed, even though that wasn't true and they gave me a brand-new one, that I kept as a spare.

We were of the same length, rank and shared the same medals, so nothing had to be altered and I gave him my brand new uniform.

On the 30th December 1944, we were given quarters in the area of Komarom. Two days later, on January 1945, we launched our first attack. Due to the fact that we didn't start with an artillery attack, the Russians were taken by surprise and we managed to take Agostyan, 76 kilometres north west of Budapest. During this attack, we lost two commanders: Untersturmfuher Hinz and….my friend Hans Heuffler. Both were killed by Russian snipers. Hinz and Hans, in order to get a better view of the territory, raised their heads to high out of their turrets. Russian snipers waited for an opportunity like this. After they shot Heuffler, his panzer was destroyed and burned out, together with my new uniform.

Achieving our advantage to Budapest, didn't come without a fight, as you may have guessed.

The Russians put PAK stands everywhere. A PAK stand, most of the time, contained eight to ten PAKs.

If we knew, by intel, there was a PAK barricade in front of us, we circled around it and attacked them from the flank. The PAKs, most of the time, were dug in, so they couldn't reposition them easily.

After destroying them with some explosive rounds, we crushed everything with the tracks of our panzers by driving over them. This was not a pretty sight, because we also drove over horses and soldiers. All that was left, was a huge amount of mince -meat. Afterwards, I inspected this carnage and I saw people with heads and bodies, squashed. Their heads looked like a run over, now flat, football.

On 2nd January 1945, we launched our attack directly at Budapest. The strength ratio at this time was already 12 to 1, sadly in favour of the Russians. Needless to say that almost all of our attacks at that time were doomed to fail. We advanced on a road and in front of us a curve appeared in that road. Immediately after this curve, a T-34 fired at our Panther. The shell ricocheted off and we responded immediately. Our round hit the T-34 in the turret. It lifted up a little bit and landed, crooked, back on the hull. A second hit from us, set the T-34 up in flames. None of the crew had time to get out of this one.

After this, we decided to leave the road and drove into a clearer area. At one point five of our panzers were driving into that clear area and suddenly, shots were fired by Russian snipers.

They were aiming at our commanders. One of our commanders didn't react quickly enough and got a bullet through his head. This panzer that was now without a commander and therefore useless in battle. In addition to this a Russian PAK started shooting and set that panzer ablaze.

Another of our panzers shared the same fate, all of the crew managed to get out alive except the driver. This was due to him going against all orders and he had closed his hatch completely, instead of putting it only on safety lock. Due to the impact of the rounds, the metal of the panzer got deformed and therefore, he couldn't open his hatch anymore. That must have created quite a state of panic in him, I guess. He managed to make his way to the side, of the radio-operator, and severely burned, crawled out and fell to the ground. As he crawled helplessly, on his hands and knees, he was shot through his leg by another sniper. After that, he didn't move anymore. He probably played dead. This was very clever, otherwise the sniper would take another shot at him.

The panzer behind him, witnessed this whole scenario, threw out fog grenades and under cover of the fog, they managed to get him out of his precarious situation.

He survived the war, but because he got gangrene in his leg, they had to amputate it and because of the severe burn wounds to his face, he was left with a very small nose and ears.

On 5th January 1945, we were transported to the city of Esztergom (50 kilometres of Budapest) to launch a second attack on Budapest. This time everything went smoothly. At least, that's what we thought. The Russians kept on pulling back and at one point, we could already see the rooftops of Budapest. Suddenly we were ordered to pull back.

Nobody understood why? We were almost there?

It became more clear after they informed us that the first commander, a general, had been executed for committing treason. They found out he gave, on purpose, false advice to his troops so they would be destroyed or defeated. Later, it turned out, we would have advanced directly into an area with countless amounts of T-34s waiting for us. The second attack therefore was postponed because of this.

Around 10th January 1945, we found, with a couple of other Panthers, quarters in Esztergom.

It came to my notice that one of the crew members of the 613, a guy named August Sievers, didn't pay much attention to his personal hygiene. He hardly washed himself. Hygiene was very important. In my infantry time, we had thousands of lice, running all over our bodies, due to the fact we hardly got an opportunity to wash ourselves. Beside the inconvenience of it, it also could cause diseases, like typhoid. Sometimes, we would put our shirts, with hundreds of lice, outside, where temperatures would drop to -45 degrees, only to find out later, if you brought the shirt back into the warmth of the bunker, the lice were still very much alive. They were more difficult to kill than Russians, I can tell you that!

After everybody washed themselves, I ordered Sievers to do also. I outranked him and so I could do this and of course he didn't. He had ignored the order. I watched him, wash himself with the cold water. He hated it, but he washed himself properly. When he came back inside, his head was red from the cold. He was lucky the commander didn't hear about his lack of hygiene, otherwise he would have given him a less savoury word on top of it.

We started our belated second attempt to make our way to Budapest on the 11th January 1945.

On the outside the city of Esztergom we bumped into the Russian army. When they saw all our panzers and infantry, panic broke out in their ranks. We helped them a little bit, with the assistance of our MGs (Machine Gun) and explosive rounds, so they knew, by now, they were not welcome here. It was probably not a very experienced unit, maybe a reserve unit, with little to no combat experience. Anyway, we made good progress that day and we conquered kilometres of terrain.

Ahead of us, we saw a Russian field kitchen, traditional horse and carriage, in blind panic running away, trying to get out of harm's way . Our commander, Alfred Grossrock, ordered 'fire' for an explosive round and because the distance was only a couple of hundreds of meters, they hit the field kitchen with the first shot. It capsized immediately, frightening the horses and they ran, with the capsized kitchen behind them, in full gallop, leaving a big trail of spilled soup behind them on the road. Yeah, I know, our humour by that time was becoming a little awkward but we had to laugh anyhow, because it was such a comical sight. We managed that day to reach the suburbs of Budapest.

On 12th January 1945, we moved on, the 613, with loader August Sievers on board, was riding in front. After a while, we heard an enormous explosion.

613 had run on to an anti-tank mine and their tracks were destroyed. It turned out to be repairable. Every Panther carried spare tracks on the side of the panzer, in case they needed them. This was like the spare tire for a car. On the backside of the 613 turret, the hatch opened and August Sievers, freshly washed again, came out. The repair was a job assigned to the loader and the radio-operator from each panzer. If they were lucky, the group of mechanics would be there quickly and then they would be excused from this heavy duty. We always hoped for that.

Sievers jumped off the back of the panzer on to the ground and the moment he hit the ground an immense explosion followed. He had jumped exactly on top of an anti-personal mine and was killed immediately. How unfortunate can you be? I had ordered him two days before, to wash himself and next he was dead. I never forgot his name, strange how your memory works.

The next day, we were transported and we arrived with our panzers in the same area where we had, had our quarters before. After that, we went back to the house where we had already spent the night before. To our surprise, our bunk area turned out to be filled with sleeping soldiers from our army. Luckily, we managed to squeeze ourselves in somewhere between all of these sleeping soldiers. We were always tired and so we also fell asleep immediately.

The next morning, we had to awake early due to the schedule for our transport and I noticed the five of us were the only ones awake? All the other soldiers were still in a deep sleep, so it seemed.

Then we found out, those others were not asleep, they were all dead! They had been killed in action and temporarily put here, until they could be buried. We spent the whole night sleeping between corpses! Not that this mattered much to us, they were our comrades.

As we were in a hurry, I forgot to check if one of these dead bodies maybe belonged to my friend Hans Heuffler. I could have said goodbye in a proper way, but unfortunately, it didn't happen.

On 18th January 1945, we started a combined operation with our sister division the 3th SS Totenkopf Division. In addition there were a couple of panzer divisions of the Wehrmacht, at our disposal.

The Wehrmacht units would be there, to cover our flanks.

To our surprise, we found out that the Russians had added electricity to the barbed wire in front of us. What were they trying to achieve with that? They thought it would scare us of? Unbelievable!

Our engineer troops quickly cut through the wire and we moved on.

We received heavy resistance on 21st January 1945, when we reached the area of Sarosd, about halfway between Budapest and lake Balaton in Hungary,.

At about this moment, the panzer, of commander Karl Heinz Lichte, was destroyed and his crew managed to get out of the panzer. Only Karl Heinz Lichte was hanging, motionless, in his turret.

The gunner managed to get out, by using the hatch of the loader, because Lichte blocked his way. We all thought Lichte was dead but Grossrock, who checked the scene with his binoculars, said: 'He's moving. He's still alive. Driver, drive to his panzer and machine gunner, shoot at any Russian infantry around that panzer.'

Meanwhile Lichte, indeed, not dead at all, managed to get out of his turret and fell to the ground.

We were only 50 metres away when I saw a Russian kneeling and aiming his gun at Lichte.

I quickly aimed with my MG34 and shot that Russian, with one burst of my MG.

Arriving at the panzer of Lichte, we threw fog grenades and in that fog we managed to get Lichte out of danger. He was unconsciousness and we transported him on the back of our panzer to medical care.

It was only in 1997, at one of our meetings that he found out that I was the only survivor of the panzer crew that saved his life. He hugged me and I received his eternal gratitude.

15
TANKS

When a panzer engages in battle, it is necessary to show your front armour to the enemy. The best position however, is to turn your front a little bit, in that way the enemy gets a slant front view on your panzer.

By doing so, you stand a better chance that enemy rounds will ricochet off your panzer. This will benefit your survival chances, so it is better to follow those guidelines. But you don't always have the chance to take the perfect position. In this case, you just hope that you're training and your weapon is better as theirs, which in many cases it was.

During the course of the war, our panzers and PAK guns grew larger barrels, but the Russian guns also got larger. A longer barrel gives a higher chance of penetrating the steel armour of the enemy. The barrel of our gun had a length of 5.25 metres. The rounds had a calibre of 7.5 cm. The shells of our rounds, however, were from the famous 8.8 gun, that was mounted, for example, on the Tiger 1 and Tiger 2. Initially the 8.8 was designed as an anti-aircraft gun, but it pretty soon turned out to have multi purposes, as a PAK, or as a panzer canon. It was one of the best and most feared guns of the 2nd WW and scared the shit out of many Allied troops.

According to an American writer about tanks, the Germans would have been better off, if they would have mass produced the Panther, instead of constantly trying to re-invent a bigger and better panzer. That only slowed down production and made the whole process complicated, instead of getting it more simplified, like it was with the Sherman and the T-34. The Panther had also some design flaws, like the fuel of the first ones easily caught fire and due to overlapping wheels, maintenance was more difficult in case of replacing an inner wheel.

Besides that, in his opinion, the Panther was the most effective panzer on the battlefield of the second WW. Of course, the Tiger 1 and Tiger 2 were formidable weapons also, but they lacked, due to their weight – horsepower ratio, speed and mobility in comparison to the Panther. Also, because we 'only' had 45 tons (Tiger 1 carried 55 tons and Tiger 2, almost 70 tons) of steel to move, our range was bigger. That is a huge benefit on the battlefield. If a tank, during battle, runs out of gasoline, it meant disaster.

Most of the time in those cases, the crew had to bail out and destroy their own panzer. Like we could afford that!

We used codename OTTO, during radio transmissions, if we needed gasoline for our tanks. In hindsight, it was ridiculous to do so, like the Russian wouldn't have a clue if a panzer unit ordered 6000 OTTO and they would being guessing 'what the hell that could mean?'

And the Russians DID listen to our radio broadcasts. I experienced it myself. Almost at the end of the war, from the 80 Panthers that we started with, we only 3 had left.

One day, one of our commanders had a little too much to drink (happened regularly), he fell off his panzer and broke his leg.

By radio, I ordered an ambulance and after I told my story of what happened, suddenly, somebody else broke in 'on the line'. It sounded to me like a German defector, because his German was perfect, and he told me; 'We had to be more careful. We didn't have many men left anymore.' He went on with his story, but I switched off my radio, without giving him any reply.

In April 1944, we started with 80 panzers. After my training, I belonged to the 6th panzer regiment of the 5th Division Wiking.

Most of us were 'baptized' during the battle of Kovel. A majority of our crew members had gathered panzer experience already during their time at the lighter panzer divisions (Panzer 1 to 4).

I told you before, that the attack formation of our panzers, was called a W formation.

Three panzers in the front, and two of them behind and in the middle of the first three. The two panzers in the front and on the outside of the W, were called 'Kettinghunde' or Chain Dogs. They were the ones that received the most of the enemy fire.

On our first mission, our position was in the top and the middle of the W.

A pretty safe position, I thought.

But my assumption turned out to be a little to positive. Entering the battlefield, the Russians started to shoot with their PAK units at our panzer. Also their artillery released a barrage of fire.

I can tell you that, during that first tank battle, I almost shit in my pants in fear.

You want to run away, and hide, but you can't go anywhere. You just have to sit and wait, while outside the whole world tries to kill you. Nothing personal, but still....

The first heavy shell impact happened right in front of me, against the sloping armour of our Panther. It was an ear deafening 'Bang' and inside the panzer, glowing sparks flew everywhere. Later on other and more experienced crewmembers, told me, these were just miniscule iron particles, released after an impact and there was nothing to worry about.

But I thought at that moment our panzer had already suffered major damage.

Well, the second shell hit us shortly after the first one, and again a hail of sparks flew through the panzer interior.

My commander informed us, it was a PAK that shot at us, and he already spotted it, and gave our gunner directions. After a few seconds a loud bang from our panzer sounded, and the sound deafened me. The commander yelled; 'Zerstort!' through his intercom, so we knew that PAK was destroyed.

The firing of a panzer canon is loud if you are sitting INSIDE the panzer, but outside it was a very vicious, sharp and hard noise. We learned to cover our ears and open our mouths, if you were so close to a canon that fired, this would equalize the air pressure and keep your eardrums intact.

We always tried to take out a PAK and their crew with ONE explosive round. That didn't always work out. Needless to say, if they were able to take a second shot at you, it could be the one that takes YOU out. So you had to be quick and perfect at the same time.

After these first hits, we had to endure many more later on, but none of those startled me as much as those first two hits, during my first battle.

Not that you got used to it, but now, at least, you knew what was going on. Those hits had, most of the time, no further consequences for the panzer except for the noise.

But if you got hit in your fuel tanks, you were in for a big bonfire and had to get the hell out of the panzer.

Most of the time, in case of burning fuel, you can still manage to get out of the panzer, but if an enemy shell would hit your ammunition, the whole panzer would explode in no-time and the chances of getting out alive are very small.

I experienced both situations, but because the driver and I were sitting in the front of the panzer, far away from the gasoline, and not many chances of a hit in our ammunition, we had the best chances of getting out alive.

Most hits were in the turret and here is also the biggest stack of rounds. Those three men, in my opinion, had the most vulnerable places of the panzer.

Also the top of the turret had thinner armour, but that was only a problem if a bomb or artillery shell should hit us directly on top. Chances were small this would ever happen, or maybe not?

This brings me to the story of Mack, he was a radio-operator, just like me, in Panther 622 or 623, I don't remember which one of them.

One day, his panzer got a direct hit on the sloped armour at the front of the panzer.

The shell ricochet off the sloped armour, bounced against the underside of the barrel and, after that, crashed on the escape hatch above Mack's head. Incredibly, it still had enough kinetic energy to smash the hatch.

The hatch broke and a piece of metal went straight into Mack's skull and killed him instantly.

Talk about bad luck. He probably never knew what hit him.

We had to wait, until after the battle, before we could get Mack's body out of his panzer.

This turned out to be a difficult job. Because he died, while sitting, his body had turned stiff, and stayed rigid in his sitting position.

So, in order to remove him, we had to break his legs to straighten him out, before we could get him out of the panzer.

Later, when we checked out the damage, we noticed a hole in the front of the panzer, were the shell bounced off, as big as a man's fist. Also the underside of the barrel had similar damage, so you can imagine what power that shell must have had, being able, after bouncing off twice, still managed to penetrate a 5 cm thick, steel hatch.

In all those years after the war, people asked me many times, if I wasn't scared. Of course, I could have bragged and said: 'Me? Never!'

But that would be far from the truth. People who state, of having no fear during battle, in my opinion, are liars or completely crazy.

Yeah, being a rookie, in the beginning of the war, I always thought nothing would ever happen to me. Later, after being wounded a couple of times, you're own mortality comes closer as never before.

I started to be more cautious taking more care of myself. Routine and caution could carry you a long way in a war.

I remember an incident, when we were in Hungary. There were four of us, enjoying a couple of days without combat.

We were crossing the field of an airport, as Russian artillery started firing. By the instinct, I gathered in all my years at the frontline, I knew from the sounds of those shells, that they would land awfully close to where we were walking at the moment

I shouted; 'Take cover' but the two guys, walking in front of me, just looked around scornful and continued their way, like nothing would ever happen to them.

The guy next to me, followed my advice and hit the ground, like me and it was not a moment too soon. 'Wham', with a thundering roar the shells hit the field, just in front of those two guys ahead of us.

They got a full load of shrapnel and both died on the spot. It pissed me off, because if they would have listened to my advice, they would still be alive. They were young and had no experience, but they thought they were invincible. Well, they were not. Their bravado caused their deaths.

Another incident, also in Hungary.

Together with my comrade Ubel, we were on our way to the field kitchen, to get us some coffee.

In front of us, it was dark already, two guys from the infantry were heading the same way. Being far behind the frontline, this should have been a stroll without any dangers.

Suddenly, we heard the sound of a so called Russian 'Nahmaschine'. The Russian Nahmachine with three little bombs is in fact a PO-2. The German troops *nicknamed* it *Nähmaschine* (sewing machine) for its rattling sound and the Finnish troops called it Hermosaha (Nerve saw).

Anyway, this plane is a very light Russian airplane, that could only carry 3 little bombs. They had to throw the bombs out of the plane by hand, for crying out loud.

The crew, flying in the dark, always tried to find lights, like from the exhaust flames of a panzer, or the lights of a truck to orientate themselves. Once spotted, they would fly to that target, drop their 3 little bombs and disappear again. At the frontlines, they never appeared, but here, behind the frontlines, you would hear them regularly.

Ubel and I just passed a little farmhouse and I suggested to go inside and wait until the plane be gone again. The other two infantry guys decided not to go inside with us.

They didn't want to take shelter inside the house. They would wait in front of the house. No shelter whatsoever.

Why? Oh well, 'It was only a little shitty plane with three little, shitty bombs', was their comment.

But being a little bomb, doesn't mean it couldn't harm or kill you.

We heard the three explosions of those 'shitty little' bombs. One in front of the house and two behind the house.

After the sound of the plane was ebbing away, we stood up (Yes, we were on the floor, even IN the house, better to be safe than sorry) and went outside. There we found out that one of those 'brave' infantry men was dead. Shrapnel of the 'little shitty' bomb, that exploded in front of the house, cut straight through his throat and he bled to dead in an instant.

Numerous times, I witnessed people losing their life, because of stupidity, carelessness or just not following the rules of safety. They all could have been alive today, if it wasn't for their behaviour.

Fear. I told you, I felt fear many times. But also I experienced mortal fear. That's different. They always tell you on a moment like that, you will see your whole life passing by. Well, I never experienced THAT, but I remember my moments of mortal fear pretty well, even after all those years.

First time, I had mortal fear, was the time I was hiding in a ditch, while a whole group of Russians passed me by. The second time was at the river Mius, also during my infantry time.

I was sitting in my foxhole, keeping very quiet, because a Russian T-34 was cruising around in our area.

Of all places, that tank decided to cruise exactly over my fox hole. I was lying there, frozen like a rabbit that looks into the headlights of a car, meanwhile seeing the tank drive over my fox hole and after that, felt the exhaust fumes of the tank blasting against my body.

They didn't know I was there, otherwise they would have zigzagged on top of my foxhole with their tracks and burry me alive.

Even my mind froze. I had no thoughts at all during those seconds.

Also the time, I was a passenger on the sideboard of our truck and we got ambushed by Russian infantry. I had to run for my life, no thoughts at all, only run.

Also the times our Panthers got destroyed and you had to get the hell out of there, if you didn't want to be cremated alive. If you managed to survive that, you next mortal fear was being shot by the Russian infantry. Your brain freezes and adrenaline kicks in: Flee or fight, and in those cases you had to flee.

So, YES, I have experienced mortal fear numerous times and NO, I never saw my whole life passing by. But maybe that's different for each and every person?

January 21th 1945, we got a medal for having participated in 50 panzer battles.

Around this time, we knew it was only a matter of time and the war would be over.

Still, we fought on. Until high command would tell us to surrender, we would be bound to our oath until our death.

On January 29th 1945, we were in the south part of Hungary, a village called Pettend, about 240 kilometres from Budapest and about 300 kilometres from the Austrian city of Graz.

It was there, that we bumped into a massive Russian tank army.

We lost a lot of panzers here, but also we had a strange incident in that town.

One of our panzer commanders, a Dutch guy named Brink, drove his Panther tank through the main street of Pettend. At the same time, without him knowing it, a Russian T-34 was driving a parallel street in the same direction as Brink.

Suddenly, at the end of the street, those two almost bumped into each other. The T-34 fired immediately at the Panther from Brink.

Brink felt the impact on his Panther, but couldn't tell where it was hit.

In an instant, he turned his turret and fired at the Russian T-34.

From this close distance, almost face to face, it was a deadly shot.

The Russian T-34 exploded and burnt out.

But at that same moment, the barrel of the gun of Brink's Panther broke off, very close to the turret, leaving him with a pathetic little canon. It was a hilarious sight.

It turned out the Russian T-34 had hit him with his shot, exactly on the barrel of his gun, knocked a part out of it, but allowed Brink just ONE shot, before it totally broke off. Brink and his crew turned out to have a very lucky moment over there.

After the battle of Pettend we only had 5 or 6 panzers left.

If you only count numbers, we never lost as many tanks as the Russians. By September 1944 they already lost more as 1000 tanks.

If the war would be decided by the numbers the enemy had lost, we would have won the war.

But, sadly, it doesn't work like that.

The workshop managed to repair a couple of our Panthers, even Brink's short nosed Panther came back with a new canon and proudly he drove away in it.

It may sounds strange, but one way or another, you get attached to that big lump of steel.

It's like your second home.

After the workshops miraculous repair work, our unit had now 10 or 11 Panthers. I don't know the exact numbers anymore, because we were not bunched together. That would make us very vulnerable.

We got intel, the Russian would launch their attack soon, so we prepared our panzers for battle. Russian artillery, as a prelude to what was coming already started to fire and we moved into the direction of that artillery fire.

There we found our infantry. For us, inside the panzer, artillery fire didn't bother us too much. Yeah, they could destroy one of our tracks or we would lose an antenna, but most of the time you would be safe inside the panzer. Only a direct hit on top of our Panther would bring us in trouble, but hey, what are the odds on that?

By now, artillery fire became very intense and we also noticed T-34's on the battlefield. Also we noticed a couple of JS tanks, (Josef Stalin tank, or the so-called IS series) that made us especially aware. This heavy tank, with a 120 mm canon, was designed with thick armour to withstand the German 88 mm gun from our Tigers and the 75 mm gun from our Panthers.

It also got a high-calibre cannon that was strong enough to fight our German Tigers and Panthers on a longer distance. We tried to keep the JS, as much as we could, on a safe distance.

The Russian tanks outnumbered us 10 to 1, so it would be a very 'cosy' day for us.

We started shooting at a distance from 2000 meters, because from that distance we could still destroy a T-34, but they couldn't destroy us.

Quickly, we destroyed one of the T-34's. The other ones started to drive nervously around all over the field, because they knew what a Panther could do to them.

Of course, tactically, you should never drive with tanks randomly around on a battlefield.

By this you made it impossible for the other tanks to have a free range of fire. You block each other. Also your vulnerable flank might get exposed.

The Russian company commander couldn't get this battle field chaos straightened out. Again, a textbook example of failing in training or lacking communication.

We managed to destroy around 30 T-34's but we lost 3 Panthers ourselves, one of them burned out, two of them had to go back to the workshop.

The Russian tanks pulled back and their artillery started firing again, causing casualties within our infantry unit.

We got the order to pull back and we did so in reverse gear. Why? Because by doing this, you wouldn't show your vulnerable backside to the enemy. Only after we knew there was no danger of being hit anymore, we turned our Panther around.

Suddenly, my commander, Alfred Grossrock, said: 'Stop, somebody is lying at the side of the road. Henk, go with Kurt and find out what's going on.'

Dusk was setting in, so it was safe enough to get out of the panzer, otherwise it wouldn't be allowed.

The guy at the side of the road, turned out to be an infantryman from the Westland division. He had a shrapnel wound in his leg. We had to be careful, because the Russian infantry was still firing at us. We managed to lift him up and place him on the back side of our panzer.

By that time he told us, there must be another wounded soldier out there.

I went out in the field and found him pretty quick.

He had a shrapnel wound in his side. He turned out to be a Dutch guy, like me and I asked him to climb on my back, as I would crawl my way to our panzer, because the artillery firing was getting more intensive by now.

This turned out to be one of the heaviest tasks, I ever had.

Crawling over the field, with a soldier on my back, who had his arms around my neck.

The driver of our panzer, saw me struggling in the field and pulled our panzer a little forward. I couldn't move anymore and out of breath, I stayed where I was, with this guy on my back.

Finally Kurt and another crewmember came to help me.

With three men, we managed to lift him on the back of the panzer also.

'Is he unconscious?', Kurt asked me.

'Not a moment ago, he wasn't', I said, and I started to talk to the guy again.

He didn't answer me. Now we examined him carefully and it turned out the guy had a terrible wound in his throat, that wasn't there when I found him.

Our only conclusion was, he had been hit by shrapnel from the artillery grenades, when I was carrying him on my back.

It cut his throat, but I stayed, miraculously, unharmed.

This guy really had bad luck but I had noticed none of it when it happened.

On march 18th 1945 we managed, while on our way to Mór, to destroy another 13 T-34's.

From that moment on we took a defensive position near the city of Stuhlweissenburg.

The city is situated between lake Balaton and Budapest in Hungary. If we lost this city, we would be in big trouble, because all the strategical roads came together on this one point.

Our commander made us a proposition: 'We have a lot of reserve crew members for the panzers, and you stayed on duty for months, without having any leave. Whoever wants to be replaced can step forward now.'

Nobody moved, not because we wanted to be heroes, or not because we were not afraid – because we were - but everybody felt the same. We couldn't accept this and leave our commander alone. No way. Dead or POW, but we decided to stay with him. One by one, he looked at us and said; 'I thank you all'.

March 21st 1945, we retreated south of Stuhlweissenburg. We had to get out of the encirclement by the Russians.

Very early in the morning of the 22nd of March 1945, we were on the move again.

By this time we only had 5 or 6 Panthers left. A fraction of the strength we started with. At daybreak we noticed a lonely JS (Josef

Stalin) tank patrolling in front of us. Luckily he was too far away to take a good shot at us.

Our journey passed by without any further troubles and I thought we would really get out of here in one piece.

I dozed off a little bit …suddenly, I awoke because of a terrible noise.

Our whole panzer was shaking and I heard our driver, Werner Kraus, shouting: 'Raus, Raus!' (Out, Out!).

I jumped up, but I forgot that my microphone and headset were still attached around my head and throat. I had to go back inside to unplug the cable and while doing that, I could already feel the heat of the flames coming towards me.

Quickly I now jumped out of the panzer, let myself glide to the ground over the sloping front side.

To avoid being shot at by Russian infantry, I crawled under the panzer to the other side and quickly jumped in one of the houses, standing next to the road.

It was here, were I met Alfred Grossrock and Werner Kranz.

Grossrock told me to go further back and try to find the truck from the mechanics, so we would have transport to our lines.

He himself wanted to go back to our panzer and check if there were more survivors of our crew.

I found out later, our loader and gunner never managed to get out. This was also the last time I would ever see Alfred Grossrock.

After the war I heard, that he was captured by the Russians. They executed him on April 5th 1945. Only 1 month before the end of the war.

We managed to find our truck and there, they informed us, we had ran into an ambush.

The Russians waited, until the 6 Panthers were on a distance of only 100 meters from their position. Then, with all guns blazing, they opened fire and destroyed our last 6 Panthers.

We managed to get back to our lines and there, they told us we were the first to make it back through the Russian lines.

Besides the driver and myself, not one of the other Panther crewmembers has survived this attack.

April 1th 1945, we retreated further, direction Austria and we crossed the Hungarian - Austrian border that same night.

We made quarter in a little village and to our surprise, next day, three Panthers and one T-34 drove into the village. The T-34 was captured by the Germans and now we used it.

These panzers only had one crew member, a driver and as they needed a full crew I immediately volunteered

Because I was only one of few radio operators, I got lucky.

All the other panzer crew members, without a panzer, were classified to the regular army.

They didn't like that at all, but there was no other choice left.

Chris Vliegen, this guy who survived, the attack in the Russian village on our truck with me, also made it this far. Later, in Dutch captivity, he turned out to be in the same prison camp as I.

Just before the village of Hatzendorf, we drew the attention of a lonely T-34.

He started to shoot at us, which was pretty stupid, because we held higher ground and with one shot we penetrated the deck of the tank and set him afire.

We moved in, just to find the Russian infantry also arrived here and they started shooting at us with machineguns.

Yeah, right, like that will help. We used an explosive round and killed them all.

The last four weeks of the war, we didn't see too much action anymore.

One incident occurred in the city Weinberg a/d Raab.

They needed our help, because the Russians conquered this little village, ransacked and raped all women in that village, even those in their 70s.

It was hardly any trouble to clear the city from the Russians. Some of them escaped with boats over the river Raab, the rest was killed by us, or captured.

As a member of the Waffen SS, you were in BIG trouble, if you were found guilty of rape. The penalties were harsh, even death penalty occurred.

I remember a Waffen SS soldier in France. He had got himself a nice French mademoiselle as a girlfriend. The woman was still married to a French guy, but hey, stranger things can happen in a marriage.

The problem started, when the French woman got pregnant from the Waffen SS soldier.

This would mean trouble in her marriage. In order to save her marriage, she told her husband, she had been raped by a Waffen SS soldier and even pointed him out.

The Waffen SS soldier was arrested, court martialled, and executed.

Later, after the war, having regrets, she admitted that she lied and posthumous he was cleared of the rape. Like that did him any good.

We went back to Hatzendorf and on the back of our panzer, a couple of infantry men settled down.

Almost at Hatzendorf, we heard a couple of explosions.

As we stopped and took a look to see the damage, we noticed the majority of our infantry men lay wounded, next to our panzer, on the ground.

On the backside of our panzer, one young soldier was severely wounded. He only moaned. He had white blond hair, still a baby face and I think, he couldn't have been more as 16 or 17 years old?

I stayed with him and held his hand. His stomach was torn open by the shrapnel, what turned out to be from those 'shitty little bombs' again, thrown out by a Russian 'Sewing Machine'.

By the time the medic arrived and took one look at the boy, he looked at me and shook his head, which meant as much as: 'Forget it, he is a goner.'

He gave the boy an injection with an overdose of morphine. I could see the boy's face turn paler and paler and then his breathing stopped and he died, while still holding my hand.

Seeing hundreds of dead men, seeing many people got killed during those 4 years, but this particular one, I never forgot.

Why? Maybe because he died on our panzer? Maybe because he was still so young and had still those boyish looks? Maybe because he died so shortly before the end of the war? I don't know. I know I still can't talk about him without breaking into tears.

Maybe for me, he stood as an example for all those friends, comrades, I have lost during all those years.

A couple of days later, we made quarter, next to a farmhouse.

I was busy, baking some potatoes, as our loader stormed into the kitchen, shouting: 'Russians!'

From the story he told us, we understood he saw in the distance three T-34's coming our way.

Our Panther stood, covered behind the farmhouse, so the Russians couldn't have spotted it, yet.

We jumped into the panzer and into position. The driver slowly drove the Panther from behind the cover of the farmhouse, far enough for us to spot the three T-34's.

The tanks of the Russians were fully loaded with infantry. Our commander went through the usual routine, distance 800 meters etcetera. The loader already put an anti-tank round in the canon, the gunner aimed and ....fire!

The first Russian T-34 was hit and stopped, now we aimed on the last one and set that one on fire. Now the tank in the middle tried to escape. Too late. Our third shot hit him in his flank and he exploded with a mighty 'Bang'.

Next we used explosive rounds for the infantry and I could empty my MG 34 on the leftovers from their infantry.

A couple of them managed to escape into the hills. All in all, this whole action, from our first shot until the last, didn't take more as five minutes.

Talk about training, discipline, and precision: we had it all!

We took a look at the crime scene and found out that, on the first tank, they had an Austrian civilian.

He told us, that the Russians asked him if he knew remaining 'Germanski' tanks in the area and they forced him to sit at the front of the first T-34 to show them the way.

The civilian had a bullet wound in his leg. Obviously I did that. This was our last act of the war. If those stupid Russians just would have stayed where they were, they would all be alive.

Now, just moments before the end of the war, they all died.

On May 8th 1945, they informed us the war was over and we had to turn over all our weapons, undamaged that is, to the Russians.

Well, we didn't follow THAT order and we blew up our last Panther, together with all the weapons and used the captured T-34 to transport us, out of harm's way of the Russians.

Of course, we wanted to surrender to the Americans and not to the Russians. Most of Waffen SS soldiers they captured were executed on the spot.

Suddenly, while passing through a little village, somebody started to shoot at us with a rifle.

War was already over, so why would somebody still wanted to kill us? No idea?

We brought the T-34 to the front of our convoy, loaded an explosive round and blew up the house were the shots came from. No more shots came back at us. Finally, peace again.

Close by, the Americans came back from Italy with all the German POW's.

We also wanted to join them as POW. No way, we would surrender to the Russians.

Our first attempt to cross the bridge and surrender to the American army on the other side, turned out to be unsuccessful.

The American guard bluntly refused to take us in. 'Go back to the Russians', he said.

Nobody wanted to follow THAT order also.

So we followed the river downstream, until we found a spot where we could wade through the river and, with no American guards at the other side, we managed to do so.

Next morning we saw trucks, full with German prisoners from Italy, on their way to a prisoner camp.

We just mingled in with them and that's how we got to be American POW's.

The POW camp was no picnic. We rarely got anything to eat and the Americans stripped us of all our medals, ribbons etcetera.

At the end of July 1945, my weight was only 55 kg, with a length of 1.80 meters (6 feet), I was mere skin and bones. Now the waiting started, to see what they would do with us?

We were interrogated a couple of times, because the Americans wanted to know if they had any members of 'Kampfgruppe Peiper' in their camp.

Later I learned, this had to do with the Malmedy massacre.

16
THE END

On October 17th 1945, I was transported, together with another 600 Dutch POW's, back to the country where I originally came from: the Netherlands.

These 600 POW's were guarded by 17 American soldiers.

The moment we crossed the border with the Netherlands, 300 guards from the B.S. (Binnenlandse Strijdkrachten or Homeland Forces) were already waiting for us.

They were all very nervous to be guarding these terrible and dangerous Waffen SS soldiers, that unfortunately one of the guards accidently fired his riffle, shot one of our men through his leg and also killed one of his own fellow B.S. guards with that same bullet.

The odds he would hit one of his own, with 300 guards to 600 POW's, was reasonably high, I guess.

From the first stop in the Netherlands, they told us, next we would be taken to a prison camp.

The Dutch navy soldiers, who were in charge from there on, treated us very correctly. Once in prison camp, as an inmate I volunteered to work, in the coalmines in the south of the Netherlands.

At least, by doing this, I earned some money, instead of doing nothing in a prison camp and wasting my time.

At court, I was sentenced to 5 years in prison, because I took service in the foreign army that my country was at war with.

Out of those 5 years, I served 3 years and in 1948, when Queen Wilhelmina abdicated the throne and gave it to her daughter Juliane, many of us got amnesty. I was a 'free' man again.

Meantime, my parents lost all their possessions. They were confiscated by the government. On top of that, they also had to do time in prison.

Why? Because they were members of the political party the N.S.B. (The National Socialistic Movement) established in 1931.

At that time, it was a legitimate political party, but they sympathized with Hitler's party, the NSDAP.

When war came to the Netherlands, in 1940, all other political parties were abolished, only the NSB became a matter of importance during those occupation years 1940 – 1945.

After the war, the cry for retribution from the people for this act of treason was high. The government of the Netherlands decided, retrospectively, to make membership of the NSB party prosecutable by law.

And so, my father and mother ended up in jail. My father's only crime, beside his membership, was to hand out pamphlets. My mother was only a member of the party and never participated in anything.

After their jail time, they had no house anymore and they were forced to live in some uninhabitable property, together with three of their grandkids and I, altogether 6 people.

We only had one room for the six of us and we had to share the toilet with the neighbours.

Because of my Waffen SS membership, I stood no chance in finding a job that fitted my education in post war Netherlands. In fact, I couldn't get a job at all. Nobody wanted us. So I decided, shortly after my release, to go to Germany.

Remember I met that nice German girl during my panzer training time in 1943 in Austria?

We still kept in contact with each other, so I decided to travel to the city of Wurzburg in Germany. Wurzburg turned out to be almost completely destroyed, like most of the German cities, by allied bombing.

On march 16th 1945 they bombed it almost completely into destruction.

Her parents lost everything and they went to live with family in the little village of Klingenberg, about 80 kilometres from Wurzburg.

I tried to find work here, but it turned out to be very difficult also.

After 5 years, in 1953, we married and we went back to the Netherlands again.

Back in the Netherlands, the tide had turned a little for the better and with the help of some friends, I got a job in a VW garage as a bookkeeper and later I worked myself up to the position of manager in a jeweller store. I worked in a jeweller store until retiring in 1987,

Sadly, I hardly knew any Dutch Waffen SS members. All my time in the service, I was in units that consisted 99% out of Germans.

I knew some names, but no addresses and many of them never came back.

Most of them were buried somewhere in Russia.

With help from my German sister-in-law, I managed to find in Germany, the associations of old Waffen SS members.

After I applied to become a member, they first checked me out to ensure that I was not a fraud and actually had been a member of the Waffen SS.

Now I finally got the chance to meet some other Dutch members too. Out of all these Dutch Waffen SS members, I did not know single one of them.

Unfortunately it would seem that the chances that you would actually find someone you served together with, was very slim, especially 40 years after the war.

I met one Dutch guy, Gerhard Magdeburg, who was two years my senior. He turned out to be in almost all the same places, I had been, had been wounded at almost the same times, even also had a shot through his leg, just like I had, sat in the same train for the wounded and ended up in the same hospital in Vienna, but we NEVER met.

It took us more than FOUR decades to figure this out. Sadly time catches up with all of us. One after another my old comrades died, due to old age.

Almost every week I got messages that so and so died, and another one and another one. The meetings became less crowded.

Also Hugo 'Honey' Schramm died and I know it will be my turn one day soon.

Note: my father died at the age of 80 years old on march 15th 2003. He left me these memories and the memory of a remarkably strong man, both in body and soul.

OVERVIEW BATTLES AND EVENTS OFF THE 6e COMPANY, 5th SS PANZERDIVISION WIKING

April 5th 1944	Attack on Dubowa – Kovel
April 6th 1944	Attack railroad Kovel – Cherkassy
April 10th 1944	Support to height 179
April 12th 1944	Tank battle height 179
April 27th 1944	Attack on Lubliniec
July 7th 1944	Tank battle north of Kruhel and counter attack height 197.2
July 8th 1944	Tank battle height 206 and 220 east of Maciejov
July 10th 1944	Defence at Maciejov, in 2 days Germans destroyed 295 Russian T-34's
July 20th 1944	Counterattack at height 178.4, Czemery
July 21th 1944	Attack at Kol-Awuls
July 22th 1944	Attack at Temienka
July 23th 1944	Battle at Nursec and Rogacze
July 24th 1944	Attack at height 180 – 178 south east of Rogacze
July 26th 1944	Counterattack railroad Biala- Podlaska to Terespol
August 1st 1944	Tank battle at Michailov
August 2nd 1944	Tank battle east of Okuniev
August 3th 1944	Advance to bridge east of Rembertov
August 4th 1944	Attack on Rembertov
August 5th 1944	Attack on Rembertov
August 6th 1944	Tank battle east of Rembertov
August 12th 1944	Attack height 105 at Lysobyki

August 13th 1944	Our panther destroyed at Lysobyki
August 14th 1944	Commander Martin killed.
August 16th 1944	Defence of Jasienica
August 17th 1944	Medal for having 25 tank battles
August 20th 1944	Our panther destroyed under an overpass.
August 21th 1944	Security of Dombrovka
August 23th 1944	Tank battle at Malapole
August 25th 1944	Tank battle at Kolakov
August 26th 1944	Security of Popowo
August 29th 1944	Tank battle Radzymin and conquered Trzciana
August 30th 1944	Tank battle at Alexandrov near Radzymin, destroyed 20 T-34's
August 31th 1944	Security Radzymin
September 4th 1944	Security Serock
September 18th 1944	Thousands of parachutes with supply for Russians ended up in our hands
September 23th 1944	Security Zakrozyn
October 10th 1944	Tank battle Nieporent
October 13th 1944	Tank battle Zegrze – Jablonna
October 15th 1944	Tank battle Zagroby
October 16th 1944	Tank battle Zagroby
October 17th 1944	Security K.Wieliszev
October 24th 1944	Tank battle Izbica
October 28th 1944	Security Dembe
Nov-Dec 1944	Battles at the rivers Bug and Narew in the wet triangle
December 26th 1944	Relocated to Hungary
January 1st 1945	Attack on Agostyan.

January 2nd 1945	2 of our tank commanders Hinz and Heufler got killed
January 3th 1945	Attack on Vertestonia. Destroyed 17 Russian PAK's
January 4th 1945	Attack on Tatabanya
January 5th 1945	Attack on Biscke stalled. Relocated to Esztergom at the Donau river
January 12th 1945	Second attack on Budapest. We had to cancel the attack.
January 13th 1945	By train to Veszprem. Regroup for a new attack on Budapest
January 18th 1945	Start of the second attack on Budapest (again)
January 19th 1945	Tank battle at Savitz canal.
January 21st 1945	Security Sarosd and we got medal for 50 tank battles.
January 22th 1945	Tank battle at Seregelyes
January 24th 1945	Tank battle at Stuhlweissenburg
January 25th 1945	Tank battle in Adony at the Donau river
January 28th 1945	Tank battle at Kajaszo and Baracska
January 29th 1945	Tank battle at Pettend. We destroyed 200 T-34's
February 2nd 1945	Tank battle at Seregelyes again
February 6th 1945	Tank battle at Dinnyes
February 8th 1945	Tank battle of Lake Velence. Security until March 16th 1945
March 18th 1945	Tank battle on the road to Stuhlweissenburg. Destroyed 13 T-34's
March 21st 1945	Our panther destroyed, lost 3 of our crew members at Nadaszdladany

April 1st 1945	Crossing Hungarian – Austrian borders
Mei 8th 1945	After some minor fights, we surrender to Americans and became POW's

17

THE 5TH SS PANZER DIVISION WIKING

The **5th SS Panzer Division 'Wiking' 5 was a Panzer** division among the thirty eight Waffen-SS divisions of Nazi Germany. It was recruited from foreign volunteers in Denmark, Norway, Sweden, Finland, Estonia, the Netherlands and Belgium under the command of German officers. During the course of World War II, the division served on the Eastern Front. It surrendered in May 1945 to the American forces in Austria.

The division took part in Operation Barbarossa, the invasion of the Soviet Union, advancing through Galicia, Ukraine. In August the division fought for the bridgehead across the Dniepr River. Later, the division took part in the heavy fighting for Rostov-on-Don before retreating to the Mius River line in November. In the summer of 1942, *Wiking* took part Army Group South's offensive Case Blue, aimed at capturing Stalingrad and the Baku oilfields. In late September 1942, *Wiking* participated in the operation aimed to capture the city of Grozny, alongside the 13th Panzer Division. The division captured Malgobek on 6 October, but the objective of seizing Grozny and opening a road to the Caspian Sea was not achieved. The division took part in the attempt to seize Ordzhonikidze. The Soviet Operation Uranus, the encirclement of the 6th Army at Stalingrad, brought any further advances in the Caucasus to a halt.

After Operation Winter Storm, the failed attempt to relieve the 6th Army, Erich von Manstein, the commander of Army Group South, proposed another attempt towards Stalingrad. To that end, *Wiking* entrained on 24 December; however, by the time it arrived on 31 December, it was forced to cover the withdrawal of Army Group A from the Caucasus towards Rostov. The division escaped through the Rostov gap on 4 February. In early 1943, the *Wiking* fell back to Ukraine south of Kharkov, recently abandoned by the II SS Panzer Corps commanded by Paul Hausser. In the remaining weeks of February, the Corps, including *Wiking*, engaged Mobile Group Popov, the major Soviet armoured force named after Markian Popov during the Third Battle of Kharkov. The losses of Popov's Group halted the Soviet offensive which followed the Battle of Stalingrad and stabilized Manstein's front.

In 1943, Herbert Gille was appointed to command the division. The SS Regiment *Nordland*, along with its commander Fritz von Scholz, were removed from the division and used as the nucleus for the new 11th SS Volunteer Panzergrenadier Division *Nordland*. The Finnish Volunteer Battalion was also withdrawn and they were replaced by the Estonian infantry battalion *Narwa*.

In the summer of 1943, along with the 23rd Panzer Division, formed the reserve force for Manstein's Army Group for Operation Citadel. Immediately following the German failure in the Battle of Kursk, the Red Army launched counter-offensives, Operation Kutuzov and Operation Rumyantsev. *Wiking*, together with SS Division *Totenkopf* and the SS Division *Das Reich*, was sent to the Mius-Bogodukhov sector. The Soviets took Kharkov on 23 August and began advancing towards the Dnieper. In October the division was pulled out of the line.

On 13 February 1945, *Wiking* was ordered west to Lake Balaton, where *Oberstgruppenführer* Sepp Dietrich's 6th SS Panzer Army was preparing for the Lake Balaton Offensive known as Operation Spring Awakening. After the failure of *Konrad III*, *Wiking* retreated into Czechoslovakia. Gille's remained as a support to the 6th SS Panzer Army during the beginning of the operation. Dietrich's army made "good progress" at first, but as they drew near the Danube, the combination of the muddy terrain and strong Soviet resistance ground them to a halt. *Wiking* performed a holding operation on the left flank of the offensive, in the area between Lake Velence-Székesfehérvár. As the operation progressed, the division was engaged in preventing Soviet efforts at outflanking the advancing German forces. On 16 March, the Soviets forces counterattacked in overwhelming strength causing the Germans to be driven back to their starting positions. On 24 March, another Soviet attack threw the IV SS Panzer Corps back towards Vienna; all contact was lost with the neighbouring I SS Panzer Corps, and any resemblance of an organised line of defence was gone. *Wiking* withdrew into Czechoslovakia. The division surrendered to the American forces near Fürstenfeld, Austria on 9 May.

Information gathered from Wikipedia

18

SS-RANKS

SS Rank	Translation of SS Rank	Wehrmacht Rank	American Rank	British Rank
None	n/a	General-Feld marschall	General of the Army	Field Marshall
SS-Oberst gruppen führer	SS-Supreme Group Leader	General oberst	General	General
SS-Ober gruppen führer	SS-Senior Group Leader	General der Infanterie, der Artillerie etc.	Lieutenant General	Lieutenant General
SS-Gruppen führer	SS-Group Leader	General leutnant	Major General	Major General
SS-Brigade führer	SS-Brigade Leader	General major	Brigadier General	Brigadier
SS-Ober führer	SS-Senior Leader	None	None	None
SS-Standarten führer	SS-Standard Leader	Oberst	Colonel	Colonel
SS-Ober sturm bann führer	SS-Senior Storm Command Leader	Oberst leutnant	Lieutenant Colonel	Lieutenant Colonel
SS-Sturm bann führer	SS-Storm Command Leader	Major	Major	Major
SS-Haupt sturm führer	SS-Head Storm Leader	Haupt mann	Captain	Captain
SS-Ober sturm führer	SS-Senior Storm Leader	Ober leutnant	1st Lieutenant	Lieutenant
SS-Unter sturm führer	SS-Under Storm Leader	Leutnant	2nd Lieutenant	2nd Lieutenant

Non-Commissioned Officer Grades

SS Rank	Translation of SS Rank	Wehrmacht Rank	American Rank	British Rank
SS-Sturm scharführer	SS-Storm Company Leader	Stabs feldwebel	Sergeant Major	Regimental Sergeant Major
SS-Standarten Oberjunker	SS-Standard Senior Officer Cadet	Oberfähnrich	None	None
SS-Haupt scharführer	SS-Head Company Leader	Ober feldwebel	Master Sergeant	Battalion Sergeant Major
SS-Oberschar-führer	SS-Senior Company Leader	Feldwebel	Sergeant 1st Class	Company Sergeant Major
SS-Standarten junker	SS-Standard Officer Cadet	Fähnrich	None	None
SS-Schar-führer	SS-Company Leader	Unter feldwebel	Staff Sergeant	Platoon Sergeant Major
SS-Unterschar-führer	SS-Under Company Leader	Unter offizier	Sergeant	Sergeant
SS-Rotten führer	SS-Band Leader	Ober gefreiter	Corporal	Corporal

Enlisted Man Grades

SS Rank	Translation of SS Rank	Wehrmacht Rank	American Rank	British Rank
SS-Sturm-mann	SS-Storm Man	Gefreiter	None	Lance Corporal
SS-Ober-schütze	SS-Head Private	Ober schütze	Private 1st Class	None
SS-Schütze	SS-Private	Schütze	Private	Private

Crew of a German machine gun

Felix Steiner, commander of the 5th
SS Wiking Panzer division

German sniper

On the railroad track advancing to Kowel

Alfred Grossrock, the commander of the Panther 611 and later the 600 of Henk Kistemaker

Panthers manoeuvring in the field

Panther of Henk Kistemaker: the 611. He could
be one of the guys standing in front of it.

The 611 behind the front lines

Another rare picture of the Panther 611 from Henk Kistemaker. He never saw these pictures himself

The 612, belonging to the same group as Henk Kistemaker

The group consisted of Panthers 611, 612, 613, 614 and 615

612 in action

The 613 with August Sievers on the left side (see his story on pages 159 to 161)

PAK in position

Henk Kistemaker in his Panzer uniform

Collateral damage of the war: a destroyed village

Panther at the railroad track to Kowel

Burned remains of the radio-operator of a destroyed Panther at the Kowel railroad.

Henk Kistemaker in infantry uniform after being wounded to his head by shrapnel

The medals of Henk Kistemaker that he left his son Peter after he died

Voordat de oorlog met Rusland begon
Staande derde van links H.K.

Picture from Henk Kistemakers personal collection: standing 3rd from left top row just before the start of Operation Barbarossa

Panther commander with closed hatch watching the area around him

Printed in Great Britain
by Amazon